Traffic Tickets.

Don't get Mad. Get them DISMISSED.

Traffic Ticket Tips, Must Knows, and Much More

By Steven F. Miller and Alexis C. Vega

Revision: October 2011

Published by:

TicketBust.com
5716 Corsa Ave., Suite 104
Westlake Village, CA 91362

ISBN: 0615551823
ISBN-13: 978-0615551821

Table of Contents

Introduction 1

Traffic Ticket Statistics 5

Traffic Tickets: Everyone Gets One...5
Number of Tickets Issued in California..6
Number of Tickets Filed in California Courts....................................6
Average Number of Tickets Contested...6
Traffic Ticket Statistics – Calculations and Sources......................7

Traffic Tickets: How To Avoid Getting One 11

Unsafe and Aggressive Driving...11
Changes in Aggressive Driving in Others......................................12
Threat of Different Driving Behaviors...12
Police Enforcement..12
Hidden Cost of a Traffic Ticket...13

So You Got A Ticket, Now What?.........................15

Know What you Were Cited for...15
Fix-It Tickets vs. Moving Violation Tickets....................................15
Overview of Common Types of Traffic Violations and the Different Types
of Tickets..16
Speeding Tickets...*17*
Red Lights and Red Light Photo Tickets.......................*20*
Sign Violations – Stop Signs and Other Signs................*22*
Cell Phone Violations...*23*
Other Violations..*25*
Truck Driver Violations...*26*

Options for Handling Traffic Tickets 28

Paying the Ticket...28
Fighting the Ticket in Court..28
Fighting the Ticket by Trial by Written Declaration.......................29

Understanding the Trial by Written Declaration 31

History of a Trial by Written Declaration.......................................31
How to determine if you are eligible for a Trial by Written Declaration...32
How to ask the Court for a Trial by Written Declaration.....................33
How to File a Trial by Written Declaration.....................................33
What to Include in a Trial by Written Declaration and What Not to
Include...37
Sample Trial by Written Declaration Statements 38

Understanding the New Trial Process...............43

Preparing for the New Trial...45
Appearing for the New Trial...46
Asking Questions..47
Speeding Violations...47
Failure To Obey Sign Violations 48
In General..48
Asking for Reductions...48
　　Speeding Tickets (and for those with a Commercial Driver's License)...49
　　Red light, stop sign, or other ticket involving a sign or signal..............49
　　Other tickets...49
Asking for Traffic School...49
Final Decision..50
Finally (A Better Way)..51

50 Traffic Ticket Tips.................................52

Tips for when you are pulled over by an officer...............................52
What not to do when you get pulled over by an officer 53
Tips for when you are caught on camera..54
Tips for when you get a speeding ticket.......................................54
Tips for when you get a stop sign ticket or red light ticket..................55
What to do after you get a ticket...55
Traffic Ticket Excuses..55

Traffic Ticket Talk Series.............................58

About TicketTalk..58
Transcripts of our Traffic TicketTalk Webisodes...............................58
　　Webisode #1 – Introduction to TicketTalk 59
　　Webisode #2 – What To Do If You Get an LA Camera Ticket: Don't
　　Ignore That Ticket...60
　　Webisode #3 – Qualifications for a Trial by Written Declaration..........61

Webisode #4 – Tips on Routine Traffic Stops 62
Webisode #5 – Where and When To File A Trial by Written Declaration
.... 63
Webisode #6 – Does an Officer Have To Show the Radar Gun? 65
Webisode #7 – Trial by Written Declaration Discussion 66
Webisode #8 – How Radar and Lidar Can Vary 67
Webisode #9 – The Statement of Fact 68
Webisode #10 – Red Light Camera Tickets 70
Webisode #11 – Let's Talk About Cell Phone Tickets 71
Webisode #12 – Commercial Drivers and Traffic Tickets 72
Webisode #13 – How to Handle Yourself During a Standard Traffic Stop
.... 73
Webisode #14 – Cell Phone Ticket Discussions Part II 75
Webisode #15 – Cell Phone Ticket Discussion Part III 77
Webisode #16 – How to Best Respond to Questions During a Stop 78
Webisode #17 – Cell Phone Ticket Conclusion Part IV 79
Webisode #18 – Continued Tips for When You Get Pulled Over 80
Webisode #19 – Discussion on Red Light Photo Tickets 81
Webisode #20 – More Tips for When You Get Pulled Over by an Officer
.... 82
Webisode #21 – Government and State Workers Part II 82
Webisode #22 – Do You Have Control Over County Seat 83
Webisode #23 – Number of Tickets Issued in California 85
Webisode #24 – Requesting a County Seat 85
Webisode #25 – Who Can Request the County Seat 86
Webisode #26 – Car Pool Violations 87
Webisode #27 – When to Ask for the County Seat 88
Webisode #28 – Parking and Stopping Infractions 89
Webisode #29 – Nevada vs. California Tickets 89
Webisode #30 – Requesting the County Seat 90
Webisode #31 – Length of Yellow Light, Red Light Camera Tickets 91
Webisode #32 – Bail Is Required With a Trial by Written Declaration. 92
Webisode #33 – How many Officers Need To Sign the Ticket 93
Webisode #34 – Better Your Chances of Getting Out of Red Light
Camera Tickets 94
Webisode #35 – One City Shuts Down Red Light Cameras 95
Webisode #36 – What To Check For On A Red Light Camera Ticket 96
Webisode #37 – What Is An FTA? 97
Webisode #38 – Is Window Tint Allowed? 98
Webisode #39 – LA City Turns Off Red Light Cameras 98
Webisode #40 – Correctable Violations 99
Webisode #41 – New Laws 100
Webisode #42 – TBD What To Include 101
Webisode #43 – New Laws Part II 102
Webisode #44 – What Not To Include In A Trial By Declaration 103
Webisode #45 – Should I take traffic school or contest traffic ticket? .. 103

Webisode #46 – Don't Just Pay A Traffic Ticket.................................*104*
Webisode #47 - Traffic School or Fight A Traffic Ticket - Part II........*105*
Webisode #48 - Traffic Ticket Points...*106*

TicketBust.com Blogs and Articles...................**108**

Past TicketBust.com Blogs..**108**

11/3/10 - 2010 Marks the Year of the First Published Case on the Admissibility of Evidence in Red Light Camera Cases.......................*108*

11/3/10 - 2010 Court Decision Could Result in Significant Number of Red Light Camera Tickets Being Dismissed.....................................*110*

11/9/10 - California Legislature Intends to Allow Street-Sweeper Automated Enforcement Systems: Assembly Bill 2567....................*110*

11/15/10 - Class Action Suit Seeks To Refund 3 Years' Worth of Red Light Camera Tickets Issued In Santa Ana, CA................................*112*

11/12/10 - What the Blank Data Fields on Your Automated Traffic Enforcement Notice to Appear Mean to You.....................................*113*

11/29/10 - Certain Group of Drivers Able to Avoid Getting Nabbed for a Red Light Photo Ticket...*113*

12/13/10 - Are Automated Traffic Enforcement Systems Speed Traps? Technically Yes! *114*

12/20/10 - Distinction Between "Rolling Right" and Straight Through Violations...*115*

12/27/10 - What LA Courts are Doing if You Don't Pay Your Red Light Camera Ticket *117*

1/3/11 - Check the Certificate of Mailing Date and Get Your Red Light Camera Ticket Dismissed...*119*

1/10/11 - Registered Owner But Not the Driver and Not Sure What to Do?...*119*

1/17/11 - Short Red Time (Late Time) on Your Camera Ticket?........*121*

1/24/11 - How to Begin Getting a Red Light Camera Ticket Dismissed *122*

1/31/11 - Be Wary of Short Yellow Lights at Camera Enforced Intersections..*123*

2/7/11 - What You Should Know About Red Light Camera Tickets...*124*

2/14/11 - Where Camera Enforced Warning Signs Are Supposed To Be *125*

2/21/11 - Will More Cities Follow Victorville's Lead?.....................*126*

2/28/11 - Benefits a Passenger can Provide if You Got a Camera Ticket *127*

2/28/11 - How to Avoid Tattling on Yourself for a Red Light Camera Violation...*128*

3/14/11 - If You're Caught on Camera for a Red Light Violation and You Were also on the Phone Can You Get a Ticket for Both? *129*

3/21/11 - Motorists Beware Camera Enforcement Systems Can Ticket For More Than Just a Red Light...*130*

3/28/11 - Improper Right or Left Turn on Green Light Can Result in Camera Ticket 130

4/4/11 - Automated Traffic Enforcement of Seat belt Law.................131

4/11/11 - Unusual Practice Used by Sacramento Superior Court for Those Wanting to Contest a Red Light Camera Ticket in Writing........132

4/25/11 - Fines for Red Light Camera Tickets Up From Last Year.....133

5/2/11 – Bicyclists and Red Light Cameras....................................134

5/2/11 – Do Cameras Shutting Down Have Any Effect on Your Current Red Light Photo Ticket?..135

5/12/11 – How to Read a West Hollywood, San Francisco Red Light Photo Camera Ticket..135

5/16/11 – What is meant by Red Time on a Camera Ticket?............137

5/26/11 – What to do When a Camera Ticket has an Unclear Photo of You..137

6/6/11 – Constitutionality of Red Light Cameras Being Scrutinized Once Again..138

6/13/11 - How Changes to Traffic School Laws Will Affect Those With Multiple Red Light Camera Tickets 139

6/20/11 - Even if LA Shuts Down Red Light Don't Forget About the One You Already Have..139

6/27/11 - Why Every Camera Enforced Intersection Doesn't Have Warning Signs Posted..140

7/4/11 - Knowing What To Include In A Trial By Declaration Statement Is Crucial For Successfully Fighting Your Traffic Ticket In The Written Form..141

7/11/11 - Why Parking Tickets Cannot be Contested Using Trial by Written Declaration..142

7/18/11 - Bicyclists Can be Cited For Red Light, Stop Signs Tickets and More...143

7/25/11 - Knowing What Not to Include In A Trial By Declaration Statement Is Just as Important For Successfully Fighting Your Traffic Ticket In The Written Form..143

8/1/11 - What to do With Outstanding Red Light Tickets For City of LA 145

8/15/11 - Speed cameras on Ramona Expressway?......................145

8/23/11 - Lower Speed Limits?..146

8/29/11 - Speed cameras on Ramona Expressway?......................147

9/7/11 - Don't Wind Up Paying for A Ticket You Didn't have to in the First Place..147

9/13/11 - Avoid High Fine Carpool Tickets 148

9/16/11 - Commercial Drivers Who Drive Too Fast Face Serious Consequences..149

Articles..**150**

Fees on Traffic Tickets Skyrocketing in California...........................150

The Ticketbuster..153

California Morning TV Anchorman Steve Schill Brings Hope to Drivers by Praising TicketBust's Traffic Ticket Service.................................*157*

Videos and Links...**159**

TicketBust.com dismissed 4 tickets for the NBC Newscaster – Click on the link to watch TicketBust.com interviewed live on NBC...............*159*

My Local Buzz TV (mylocalbuzztv.com) features TicketBust.com as the the company leading the way assisting driver's to contest their traffic tickets by using a California Trial by Written Declaration. They state it's the best way to contest a traffic ticket in California..........................*159*

Steve Miller, CEO, speaks on KFWB News Talk 980 AM on the Penny & Phil Show Providing His Expertise on Contesting Traffic Tickets.......*159*

Steve Miller, CEO, speaks on the Karel Show as an expert on traffic tickets for Energy 92.7 FM..*160*

BBB Interviews TicketBust.com to Inform Public of Legal Rights Concerning Fighting Traffic Tickets - Click on the link to read full story
....*160*

TicketBust.com - "A Better Way To Fight A Traffic Ticket" - Dog Lover
....*161*

TicketBust.com - "A Better Way To Fight A Traffic Ticket" - Hottie TV
....*161*

TicketBust.com - "A Better Way To Fight A Traffic Ticket" - Business Woman..*161*

TicketBust.com - "A Better Way To Fight A Traffic Ticket" - Plumber.161

TicketBust.com - "A Better Way To Fight A Traffic Ticket" - Handyman
....*161*

TicketBust.com - "A Better Way To Fight A Traffic Ticket" - Business Man...*161*

Introducing iTicketBust – The first mobile APP to contest and dismiss your California Traffic Ticket – AND IT'S TOTALLY FREE...............*161*

Definitions to Commonly Used Traffic Ticket Terms **162**

Introduction

There's little question that driving is a necessity in California. Whether you drive for work, just to drop the kids off at school, or for pleasure, you need to drive. And driving responsibly requires a valid driver's license and auto insurance. However, it's a rare individual who steps into their car and hits the road without thinking of the potential dangers of getting a:

"Traffic Ticket!!!"

Just hearing those words makes people angry, worried, scared and unsure about what to do. Most people don't know what their full range of options are when they get a ticket, so they usually end up paying the fine, accepting the additional point on their driving record and the increase in their insurance premiums. And, with as expensive as auto insurance is already, who needs to pay more for it?

So, what can you do when you receive a traffic ticket? Do you just have to pay it? Well, you can always take a day off from work or school, trudge down to the courthouse and try to contest the ticket; but what good will that do? You're not an attorney, how can you expect to present your case effectively in front of a judge especially when the officer who gave you the ticket is going to be there telling the judge what you did wrong?

There must be other options. Sure you can take traffic school, but who wants to waste eight or more hours of time in a class, or online, listening to a boring instructor drone on and on about traffic rules and related topics, or watching videos of car crashes? And, if you do go to traffic school, you can't go again for another 18 months; so you better not get another ticket.

Well, that's why we are here. At TicketBust.com, we're going to help you successfully fight your traffic ticket! Using easy to follow, step-by-step instructions, you can fight and win! Keep your driving record clean, prevent points from going on your driving record and keep your auto insurance rates low!

In fact, every driver has certain rights. And, one of these rights involves a very simple option for fighting traffic tickets other than a court trial or traffic school. Drivers who get ticketed can file what is commonly called a "Trial by Written Declaration" to contest a traffic ticket without going to court or taking traffic school. A "Trial by Written Declaration" is a form that you fill out explaining the circumstances surrounding your ticket, including why you received the ticket and why you believe that you're innocent of the traffic infraction for which the officer ticketed you.

The information in this book will provide you with the knowledge, tips and trade secrets you need to be aware of in order to fight your traffic tickets and win. We will also provide you with our Top 50 Tips for what to do if you get pulled over for a traffic violation, some statistics about traffic tickets and an overview of the most popular traffic violations. We also will provide you with helpful links and other relevant information regarding traffic tickets in California.

About TicketBust.com TicketBust.com has been around for over seven years, helping drivers contest their traffic tickets and, in many cases, get those tickets dismissed. We have contested over 30,000 tickets in California and are sharing the information and knowledge acquired during those years with you. We don't believe that you need to just roll over and pay that traffic ticket. You have options and we are here to help you with those options.

You can also visit our web site at www.TicketBust.com for additional information. For Spanish you may visit www.combatesuticket.com and for cell phone ticket please visit www.fightcellphoneticket.com. You may also download iTicketBust, our mobile application for iPhone and Android devices. This is the only mobile application that will let you take a picture of your traffic ticket, input all your information and submit it to www.TicketBust.com to help you contest your traffic ticket

About Steven F. Miller Founder and president of TicketBust.com, Steve is the driving force behind the success and growth of TicketBust.com. Steve started TicketBust.com in 2004 with one goal in mind, to help drivers contest and dismiss their traffic tickets. Since then, Steve has continued to expand TicketBust.com by developing and deploying the necessary solutions to continue to assist drivers with contesting their traffic tickets.

In 2010 Steve released www.combatesuticket.com to assist the Spanish speaking community along with www.fightcellphonetickets.com to specifically address the needs of drivers receiving cell phone tickets. Most recently in 2011 Steve wanted to make it more convenient for drivers to immediately contest a traffic ticket so iTicketBust, a mobile application for iPhone and Android devices, was released.

Prior to TicketBust.com, Steve was CEO of MediaHippo, Inc., an interactive agency focused on web, DVD, and multimedia development. Steve graduated from California State University Northridge, with a BS in Accounting. Steve worked for Deloitte Haskins and Sells as a Certified Public Accountant, prior to starting his own accounting agency. Steve was instrumental in promoting and marketing the Kodak Photo CD technology in the 1990's, authored many articles and was a featured speaker at many industry events.

About Alexis Vega While in her second year of Law School Alexis joined the team at TicketBust.com. Because of her unique background Alexis was interested in working with a company that specialized in helping people contest and dismiss their traffic tickets. Coming from a family with several members in law enforcement, Alexis had a special interest in the area of traffic tickets and inside knowledge about traffic laws and traffic enforcement. Her father is a retired California Highway Patrol Lieutenant and she gained a great deal of knowledge from him, as well as from her other immediate family members that were employed by various law enforcement agencies including the Glendale Police Department, Ventura Police Department, and the California Highway Patrol.

While completing her degree, Alexis also gained extensive experience while working as an intern at various courts in Ventura County, including the Superior Court of California Office of the Public Defender where she assisted with trial preparation and the California Court of Appeal researching and writing memorandum for the Appellate Justices. Alexis was also an intern at the Law Offices of Ronald G. Harrington and Associates, where she assisted with Pro Bono case files.Alexis graduated from The Colleges of Law, Santa Barbara and Ventura, with the degree of Juris Doctor.

During her first few months of employment at TicketBust.com she helped to develop new strategies to help drivers get their traffic tickets dismissed; a continuing goal of hers. Alexis is now the Senior Case Consultant at TicketBust.com and uses her knowledge and experience to help train and mentor other Case Consultants.

Traffic Ticket Statistics

Traffic Tickets: Everyone Gets One

We've all experienced that same sinking feeling...sitting by the side of the road, in complete shock at what just happened. You've just received a speeding ticket. You can't believe it! After driving that exact same route for years, back and forth to work, [school, church, a relative's house, etc.] without ever having had a second thought that you might have been breaking the law. You have always just kept up with the flow of the traffic around you. At that point, you, like most people, will think: "Well, why didn't he pull over the guy next to me? He was driving in the fast lane and going much faster than I was?"

Your next thought might be, "Oh my gosh, my wife [husband, Mom, Dad, etc.] is going to hit the roof [kill me, take away my car keys, ground me, etc.]". "The last thing I need right now is the added expense of paying a speeding ticket". Of course, you have no idea how much a speeding ticket costs these days. Then you recall stories you have heard from co-workers [fellow students, neighbors, family, etc.] about how horrible their experience was with the outrageous fines, points on their driving record, raised automobile insurance premiums. Or their stories about fighting the ticket in court, having to stand before the judge, facing off with the officer that cited them and losing anyway. Not to mention, having to take the day off from work or school, and confessing to their employer that they had broken the law.

Whether you're a repeat offender or it's your first time, you're not alone; just about everyone receives a ticket at least once in their life. Actually, most people receive at least one ticket every year.

Below are some traffic ticket statistics that may surprise you. Keep in mind that some of the numbers below are just estimates and forecasts and may not reflect real life numbers.

Number of Tickets Issued in California

Number of Traffic Tickets Issued Yearly in CA in the Millions (includes all types of traffic tickets whether misdemeanor or infraction, parking, and administrative tickets that are never filed with a court):

2008 - 17.1

2009 - 17.3

2010 - 17.8

2011 - 18.3

Number of Tickets Filed in California Courts

Number of Traffic Tickets Filed in CA Superior Courts (includes only traffic infractions and local ordinance violation cases that are filed with a court):

2008 - 6,072,131

2009 - 6,132,852

2010 - 6,194,181

2011 - 6,256,123

Average Number of Tickets Contested

Average number of traffic tickets contested in California Superior Courts in one year (whether in person or written; includes misdemeanors and infractions):

Approx.: 1,693,600; About 9% of the roughly 18 mil traffic tickets issued a year are actually contested.

Average number of traffic tickets contested in California Superior Courts via in person court trial in one year (includes misdemeanor and infractions):

Approx.: 1,270,200; 75% of those traffic tickets contested in court are in person trial.

Average number of traffic tickets contested in California Superior Courts via Trial by Written Declaration in one year (includes misdemeanor and infractions):

Approx.: 423,400; 25 % of those traffic tickets contested in court are through a Trial By Written Declaration.

Traffic Ticket Statistics – Calculations and Sources

Year Trial By Written Declaration started in CA

1978 [source – Superior Court CA case *People v. Kennedy*, filed 12/4/2008, Super. Ct. Nos. ACRAS800066 & 2694973MK]

Number of Traffic Tickets Issued in CA (includes all types of traffic tickets whether misdemeanor or infraction, parking, could also include warning tickets given):

Approx.: 16 mil in 2007 [- source – http://wiki.answers.com/Q/How many tickets issued in California per year #izz1DUSGXdw; http://www.lectlaw.com/files/crs09.htm;California Parking Violation Laws, By Matt Margrett, eHow Contributor, July 29, 2010 – "As of January 1 2010, there were more than 23 million licensed drivers and almost 32 million registered vehicles in California. This is more vehicles than in any other U.S. state, so it is not surprising that in California's courts there are more than 15 million traffic violations filed each year. Read more:

California Parking Violation Laws | eHow.com http://www.ehow.com/list_6794200_california-parking-violation-laws.html#ixzz1LJqbAH2a]

2008 – 17.1 (CHP tickets increased 1.07 from 07 so predict same increase here)

2009 - 17.3 (CHP tickets increased 1.01 from 08 so predict same increase here)

2010 - 17.8 (CHP tickets increased 1.03 from 09 so predict same here)

2011 – 18.3 (avg. increase over years is 1.03 so use this here to predict)

Number of Traffic Tickets Filed in CA Superior Courts (includes only traffic infractions and local ordinance violation cases):

2004 - 5,669,611 [source - Court Statistics Project, State Court Caseload Statistics, 2004 (National Center for State Courts, 2006)]

2005 - 5,810,121 [source - Court Statistics Project, State Court Caseload Statistics, 2005 (National Center for State Courts, 2007)] (divided current year by prior year = 1.02)

2006 - 5,928,507 [source - Court Statistics Project, State Court Caseload Statistics, 2006 (National Center for State Courts, 2008)] (divided current year by prior year = 1.02)

2007 - 6,075,208 [source - Court Statistics Project, State Court Caseload Statistics, 2007 (National Center for State Courts, 2009)] (divided current year by prior year = 1.02)

2008 - 6,072,131[source - Court Statistics Project, State Court Caseload Statistics, 2008 (National Center for State Courts, 2010)] (divided current year by prior year = 1.00)

2009 - 6,132,852 (previous year X 1.01)

2010 - 6,194,181 (previous year X 1.01)

2011 - 6,256,123 (previous year X 1.01)

Number of Traffic Tickets Contested in CA Superior Courts via in person Court Trial:

Approx.: 1,270,200 [source – Trial Court Supervisor Traffic Division, Northwest District LA] Formula: Approx.: 60 court trials in a day, of 60 there are 40 in person, 20 TBD. 60 X 365 = 21,900 traffic tickets contested a day X 58 trial courts = 1,270,200

Number of Traffic Tickets Contested in CA Superior Courts via TBD:

Approx.: 423,400 [source – Trial Court Supervisor Traffic Division, Northwest District LA] Formula: Approx.: 60 court trials in a day, out 60 there are 40 in person, 20 TBD. 20 X 365 = 7,300 TBD's read a day X 58 trial courts = 423,400

Percent of Traffic Tickets Contested Compared to Number of Tickets Filed in One Year:

Approx. 27%: (Formula: Avg. # contested by in person or written 1,693,600/   Avg # of traffic tickets filed 6,163,822 = .27 X 100 = 27%

Percent of All Traffic Tickets Contested Via Trial by Written Declaration:

25 % (Formula: Avg. # TBD 423,400 / Avg. # contested by in person or written 1,693,600 = .25 X 100 = 25 %

Percent of Traffic Tickets Contested by Trial by Written Declaration vs. In person:

Approx.: 33%

(Formula: Approx.: 60 court trials in a day, of 60 there are 40 in person, 20 TBD. 20 X 365 = 7,300 TBD's read a day X 58 trial courts = 423,400

423,400 /1,270,200 = .33 X 100 = 33%)

Traffic Tickets: How To Avoid Getting One

How can you avoid receiving a traffic ticket?

While who gets ticketed and for what reason may seem completely random, it actually isn't. A quick study of the most common tickets will reveal certain patterns that you can learn to avoid, greatly cutting down on your chances of getting a ticket.

Below are some interesting traffic ticket statistics that may get you to rethink your own driving habits and make some modifications so that you do not become just another statistic. (Note: some of this information was adapted in part from material found at TrafficViolationLawFirms.com).

Unsafe and Aggressive Driving

Unsafe behaviors, not classified as speeding, make up a sizable portion of vehicular crashes. Drivers reported doing unsafe and aggressive driving behaviors "at least sometimes." These behaviors include but are not limited to:

- Entering an intersection just as the light turns from yellow to red (40 % of drivers polled);

- Rolling stops at stop signs (30% of drivers polled);

- Making angry, insulting, or obscene gestures towards another driver (12% of drivers polled);

- Cutting in front of other drivers (10% of drivers polled);

- Drivers age 21 and younger are much more likely than older drivers to engage in these behaviors, with 29% saying they cut in front of other drivers, 24% making obscene or angry gestures towards other motorists, and 17% using the shoulder to pass in heavy traffic.

Changes in Aggressive Driving in Others

Drivers polled believe that other drivers are more aggressive now than they were one year ago. More specifically, compared to a year ago, 40% of drivers feel that other drivers are driving more aggressively; while 52% of drivers feel other drivers are driving as aggressively as previously. Only 6% feel other drivers are driving less aggressively.

Threat of Different Driving Behaviors

While speeding was the biggest unsafe driving behavior, drivers polled were asked about other unsafe driving behaviors with regard to their personal safety.

- Virtually all drivers (97%) felt that when other drivers run red lights it is a major threat to themselves and their family.
- 83% felt that traffic weaving is a major threat.
- 58% saw rolling stops at stop signs as a major threat.

Police Enforcement

Not including speeding, polled drivers believed that enforcement was too lax with the other unsafe driving behaviors. With 60% of drivers polled believing that there is too little enforcement for tailgating and 57% believing there is lax enforcement for weaving.

Younger drivers are most likely to believe there is too much enforcement for most of the unsafe driving behaviors, especially speeding; 22% of those under age 30 reported that they believe there is too much police enforcement of speeding, as compared to 8% of those age 30 or older.

Hidden Cost of a Traffic Ticket

We recently heard from one of our potential new clients of yet another cost of getting a speeding ticket. In addition to all of the other hidden costs of a speeding ticket that we've covered previously, this driver shared with us that the main reason he was looking for help was because he lost a promotion over a previous ticket on his record and had just recently been cited again. Bringing to our attention another area to include on our previous list of the hidden cost of speeding tickets.

Here is his story. This gentleman works for a Fortune 300 company in a management position. Last year, there was a promotion for a higher level management spot and he was in the running. Unfortunately, the Hiring Manager for the position pulled driving records as part of the screening process. The other employee in the running won out because he had a 'cleaner' record! The Hiring Manager cited the fact that sometimes the position required driving a company car and that they did not need the added potential liability that may be caused by a driver with more "points" than the other candidate. What price tag can one place on losing a promotion due to a few speeding or traffic tickets?

Therefore, our "new" list of the hidden costs of a speeding ticket is as follows:

1. Potential negative impact on employment.

2. Potential negative impact on memberships to any institutions that may gauge character on your driving record or perform a background check on you.

3. Added points to your driving record. Once these points add up to a certain amount, your driving privileges can be revoked.

4. Higher automobile insurance premiums. According to insurance companies, one in four US drivers will get a speeding ticket in the coming year. Of course, the

more you drive, the greater the odds are of you being that one in four. The reason? Virtually every single one of us drives faster than the posted speed limit on most roads — because the posted speed limits are invariably set anywhere from 5-10 mph or more below the natural flow of traffic on any given road.

5. Time off work if you choose to try and fight your ticket in court.

6. Fees for traffic school if you choose to (and are eligible to) opt for this route.

So You Got A Ticket, Now What?

Know What you Were Cited for

The first step in determining your best, most effective approach to fighting your ticket is determining what, exactly, you were cited for. Not all tickets are equal. Some can even be fixed with little effort and a small fee.

In the next section we'll explain what types of tickets can be corrected, or fixed (commonly called a "Fix–It Ticket") and how to go about this.

Fix-It Tickets vs. Moving Violation Tickets

Speeding, red light, stop sign, cell phone use, and unsafe lane change tickets are generally NEVER correctable. Tickets for not having proof of insurance, or your front license plate mounted, etc., generally ARE correctable, but still involve you spending considerable amounts of time getting the problems corrected.

Here's how to tell if your violation is correctable. Check your ticket in the same area that you find the violation code: generally right around the center of the ticket. There are boxes on the left side and if the "Yes" box is checked then this violation is correctable.

If you were cited for not having "Proof of Insurance" but you DID have an insurance policy at the time, then your violation should also be eligible for correction; even if the "Yes" box isn't checked. Showing your current insurance to the court will correct this problem.

For all correctable violations you will need to send whatever documentation you have as your "Proof of Correction" to the court. This proof simply shows that the violation was fixed and you are no longer in violation, along with the fee the court assesses. The assessed fee will be on the courtesy notice sent to you by the court, but you can always call the court to find out or confirm the amount. Usually it will be a nominal fee of around $25.00.

If you are not sure what types of documents can be considered as a "Proof of Correction", here are some examples:

- Car repair receipt
- Registration documents
- Insurance documents
- Copy of Driver's License

Once you have these documents, take them and your ticket to any law enforcement office and ask them to sign off on the correction. The sign off area will be on the back of the ticket. Make a copy for your records and mail both documents back to the courts.

Tickets for a moving violation are generally not eligible for correction.

So, you now have a decision to make: will you fight the ticket or just pay the fee and accept the points on your record and increased insurance premiums? Before making any rash decisions, keep reading to learn about the different types of tickets you can receive and tips on how to fight them.

Overview of Common Types of Traffic Violations and the Different Types of Tickets

Picture yourself in this same predicament that so many of your fellow drivers have been in at one point in their lives. You were ticketed by an officer (or received an unpleasant surprise ticket in the mail with your picture on it thanks to a red light camera), but you really have no idea what the officer is saying you did!

In this chapter we'll comb through the most common types of traffic tickets out there and debunk some common misconceptions.

Speeding Tickets
I was going with the flow of traffic so I shouldn't have been stopped and issued a ticket right? Wrong! If you think, or think you've read, that going with the flow of traffic is a sure way to make sure you won't get a ticket, you couldn't be more wrong. The truth is, going with the flow of traffic is no excuse for a speeding ticket, so don't plan on using that as your only defense to try and get out of your speeding ticket.

However, if there was a legitimate emergency situation that caused you to speed up you may have a good shot. Imagine this scenario: you're driving down a steep hill on the freeway at night and you glance in your rearview mirror to see headlights weaving and rapidly approaching your vehicle. You fear you are going to be rear ended so you speed up to get around the car in the lane to your right so that you can move out of the left lane and away from the erratically driven vehicle. This is the type of situation judges don't mind listening to and if they believe your story they can order the ticket be dismissed. What judges don't want to hear is that you drank a large smoothie and had to speed up to get the next gas station so you could use the bathroom.

The difference here is that in the first scenario you sped up to avoid harm. Speeding up to avoid harm to yourself or others is something most judges want to hear about.

Maybe you were ticketed for exceeding the maximum speed limit on a California freeway or on a city street. In order to be pulled over and cited on a freeway, all that needs to be proven is that you went over whatever the posted maximum speed limit is for that freeway (55 mph, 65 mph, or 70 mph). So, your goal here is to try and prove the officer couldn't have been right about your speed. Isn't it possible that that officer didn't have a clear view of your car? Or, that the radar gun the officer used wasn't calibrated recently? Either instance can result in genuine human error on the part of the officer. Why should you pay for someone else's mistake?

If you've received a ticket for speeding on a city street what you are being cited for is generally "unsafe speed". In this case you want to gather as many details as you can about the area in which you were cited. Your specific surroundings at the time you got the ticket will definitely impact a judge's determination of whether your speed was safe or not. You can imagine a judge will be a lot more understanding if you went a little too fast on an empty country road versus a little too fast on a busy street near a school that was in session.

If, when approached by the officer who has pulled you over, he mentions that he "clocked" you exceeding the speed limit, that must mean he used radar, right? Wrong! the term "clocked" can be used to refer to several types of methods an officer can use to estimate your speed. Some of these methods are outlined in greater detail below.

Aside from just "eye balling" your speed, an officer can use a radar or laser gun, can just follow you with his patrol vehicle and note the speed at which you're both traveling, or the officer may partner up with another officer in an airplane and get a determination of your speed that way. In order to properly fight your ticket you've got to know which method the officer used. Here are some tips for figuring out what method the officer used.

Radar If the officer used a radar gun when estimating your speed, then there should be a serial number written on the ticket indicating which gun the officer used. You'll be able to tell if it was a radar gun because radar serial numbers usually start with "DC", "AT", "AS", or just a set of numbers with no letters. The serial is usually in two sets. For example: DC123/456 or 1234/5678. Radar can also be used in moving mode whereas laser can't. So if the officer was driving in the opposite direction from you, you can bet radar was used. It is very important for you to know that radar is most accurate and effective when the officer has a clear line of sight and there is not a lot of traffic.

Laser/Lidar Laser and Lidar are terms that are used interchangeably. An officer can look through a scope on a laser device or through binoculars to view a vehicle, then place a red dot on the vehicle within the scope and pull the trigger. Laser allows an officer to pinpoint vehicles easier than radar but the officer still needs a clear line of sight to do this. To spot whether a laser device was used to measure your speed, look on your ticket and check for the serial number. It will usually start with "T/S or "U/X". The officer may also help you out by writing an "L" in the middle of the ticket with a circle around it under the description section on a ticket. There are no moving laser units.

Pace When an officer follows you from behind your car as it is traveling and notes the speed at which you're both moving. Generally the officer will write from "Point A" to "Point B" near the location section on a ticket. Another way to tell is the patrol vehicle number will be circled and there will be a line through the radar/lidar section of a ticket.

Visual This is "eyeballing". The officer didn't use any device or partner and didn't follow you as your car was driving. Generally the radar or laser boxes on a ticket are left completely blank and there are no serial numbers written on the ticket. For example: the ticket will just say "s/b Hacienda/Los Altos" in the section for location.

Aircraft An officer in a plane is clocking your vehicle from the air. The officer in the plane radios a ground officer to pull your car over and issue a citation for speeding. Generally the ground officer will write "plane" or "air" on the ticket in the space for radar.

Working Together An officer might use any combination of methods to measure your speed and may also be working together with another officer to measure your rate of travel. One officer will "clock" you and the other is directed over the radio to pull you over. Even if the officer doesn't tell you specifically that he was working with another officer, if you check on your ticket and see the names of two different officers on your ticket, then you know they were working together.

Generally speaking, those are the different ways an officer might estimate your speed. Red light tickets are a different story and we discuss those next.

Red Lights and Red Light Photo Tickets
You can be ticketed by an officer or by a red light camera, and whichever way you slice it, neither one is pleasant. Below, we will discuss what things you should do, or keep notes of, to help you in fighting your ticket.

If you were ticketed by an officer be sure to take note of the traffic and weather conditions at the time you were pulled over. Also note where the officer was in relation to your car at the traffic light. Often times the officer was driving in the opposite direction and couldn't even see the color of the light you were facing, or there may have been cars in between you and the officer. If the officer didn't have a clear view of your car at the light how can he be so sure you ran it? Take lots of pictures and make a diagram, if you can. If you had a witness with you at the time, even better! Have your witness write a witness statement for you and get it notarized. A witness statement can be immensely helpful in fighting your ticket. This is true for whether you got ticketed by an officer or by a camera.

Speaking of those pesky cameras, a lot of guidelines and rules have to be followed for your infraction to even be considered a valid ticket by the court.

Here are the main things to look for:

- If you are the registered owner of the vehicle and the ticket was not mailed to you within 15 days of the date of the violation then you should be able to get it dismissed.

20

According to the California Vehicle Code section 40518 (a) "a written notice to appear based on an alleged violation of VC§21453 must be delivered to the registered owner within 15-days of the violation". This probably won't work if you and your spouse are both registered owners and it was sent to your spouse first and then put into your name afterwards.

- If the photo of the driver is either blurry or clearly not you, you should be able to get a dismissal based on there being a lack of proof beyond a reasonable doubt that it was you driving the vehicle.

- Were there any reasons why it wasn't completely safe to stop your car? Was there a situation that could have caused an accident had you stopped and not triggered the red light camera? For example, was the pavement wet or was a car tailgating behind you? Take note of any reason as to why it wasn't safe to stop; maybe you couldn't see the light due to some obstruction like the sun, or a tall vehicle ahead of you, and by the time you could, it was too late.

- Dig around and find out if there is a contract between the red light camera company and city in which you were issued the ticket and find out if it was signed or amended after January 2004. If so, call down to City Hall and see about getting a copy of the contract. If the payment arrangement between the city and the camera company is not completely "flat rate" and allows for payment to the camera company to be based on how many tickets are issued, you should be able to get the ticket dismissed (see California Vehicle Code Section 21455.5 (g)).

- More digging: also contact City Hall or the City Manager and find out where you can get the documents showing when Warning Tickets were sent out for all the camera enforced intersections in the city, including where you were ticketed, and when there was a Public Announcement for the city's camera system. If there were no warning notices sent at all, or warning notices were sent but not for every camera installed in the city, or there was no public announcement made, then you should be able to get the ticket dismissed. (see California Vehicle Code Section 21455.5(b) and 21455.6(a)).

- Keep on digging...now try and find out if there are warning signs posted at the intersection where you got the ticket. If there aren't warning signs for all of the approaches to that intersection, then you'll have to do some research and find out if there are signs posted at all main entrances to the City. If not you should be able to get the ticket dismissed. (see 21455.5(a) (1)).

- Alright, you're probably sick of digging by now, so here's the last thing you should check for. Check with City Hall or try the City Manager and find out where you can get copies of the written guidelines that are supposed to be in place for the screening and issuing of tickets from the photographs taken by the camera. If there are none or the guidelines are substandard then you should be able to get the ticket dismissed. (see California Vehicle Code Section 21455.5(c) (1)).

Next we go on to discuss those pesky tickets for different types of signs.

Sign Violations – Stop Signs and Other Signs
Traffic signs are everywhere. They tell us where to stop or where to slow down. Where we can turn and where we can't turn. Where we can park and where we can't park (and during what hours we can or can't park there!). These types of signs are everywhere. We've all seen 'em. Even more of us have "failed to obey" them because nine times out of ten we just plain didn't see the sign! It doesn't seem like there is any way to get out of this right? Wrong! Tickets for "failing to obey a sign" are generally cited under California Vehicle Code Sections 21461 or 22101 and there are ways to beat them!

What you want to do right away is go back to the scene of the ticket and look for the supposed sign. Take pictures of it. Note the weather and traffic conditions at the time. Note how far away the officer was when you first saw him. The reason for all this information gathering is because by doing it, you will probably find some reason as to why the sign didn't come into your view. Maybe the sign was posted very high up and you wouldn't have thought to look up that high. Maybe it was too dark to see and you weren't familiar with the area. Maybe there was very heavy traffic and there were taller vehicles around you that blocked it. Maybe there were overgrown trees covering the sign. Or maybe you were all the way over on the left lane and the sign was posted all the way over on the right.

Whatever the reason may be, more often than not, there is a perfectly valid excuse as to why you couldn't or didn't see the sign and if you can put together a diagram and description, or get photographs, or even have a witness testify on your behalf, you have a good chance at getting a judge to understand why the ticket should be dismissed. Similarly there are ways to have cell phone ticket dismissed which we discuss next.

Cell Phone Violations
Take two motorists, Driver A and Driver B. Both driving along and each one gets a call on their cell phone. Both drivers accept the call but Driver A puts the call on speaker and keeps the phone in his hand. Driver B just holds the phone to her ear. Both are spotted by a police officer. Who gets the ticket? Driver A? Driver B? Both Drivers? The correct answer is both drivers. In actuality, it is a common misconception that you will only get a cell phone ticket if the phone is RAISED to your ear.

Under California Vehicle Code Section the specific criteria for being cited includes if you are having a conversation on speaker phone and the phone is in your hand or if you are having a conversation with your Blue Tooth on and you have the phone in your hand because that means that you are not fully hands free. Technically you are only breaking the law if you are making or receiving a call and are driving with the phone in your hand. However, you should still expect to get pulled over anytime an officer sees a cell phone in your hand. The officer just looks into your car and sees a phone in your hand and has to assume you are talking at the same time. Don't put yourself in this situation. Keep the time your phone is in your hand to an absolute minimum; for example if you have to search for a name in your address book, or dial a number, or change the song you are listening to.

If you do get a ticket and the officer was actually wrong you can always contact your wireless service provider and obtain a copy of your call records for that day to show no calls were made or received at the time of the ticket. If you were in the wrong, it's not necessarily a lost cause. Don't get your call records, instead turn the tables. If the officer doesn't have your call records to prove you were on the phone, what kind of solid evidence does he have against you? Since the officer is not getting paid extra to write down his testimony in a Trial by Written Declaration, it is unlikely he will subpoena your cell phone carrier for those records. You can also always work in facts such as the officer's view being obstructed and not seeing clearly into your car.

If you get a ticket for texting (California Vehicle Code 23123.5) instead of talking on the phone then you also need to know the following: the current texting law only makes it illegal to use a cell phone to manually communicate with any person using a text-based communication. There are many uses other than that, that may make it appear that you were texting to a passing officer (like typing in an address for directions or browsing the web) but if you were typing something into your phone for a reason other than to "manually communicate with another person" then the law is on your side. If you were actually texting or emailing somebody, then keep the same principles in mind that we discussed in the first few paragraphs of this Chapter.

Other Violations

We've been discussing the most common types of violations but what about those that are not so common? There are definitely ways to deal with those as well. Here's what we suggest:

First look up the vehicle code you were cited for. It's easy to look up on www.leginfo.ca.gov. Click on "California Law". Then Click on "Vehicle Code". Type in the code section (numbers only) that the officer wrote on your ticket. Scan through the code section to pick out those key phrases that make up the elements of the offense.

For example, this is the description for failing to stop for a school bus:

> 22454. (a) The driver of any vehicle, upon meeting or overtaking, from either direction, any school bus equipped with signs as required in this code, that is stopped for the purpose of loading or unloading any schoolchildren and displays a flashing red light signal and stop signal arm, as defined in paragraph (4) of subdivision (b) of Section 25257, if equipped with a stop signal arm, visible from front or rear, shall bring the vehicle to a stop immediately before passing the school bus and shall not proceed past the school bus until the flashing red light signal and stop signal arm, if equipped with a stop signal arm, cease operation.

This is the description again, but this time notice the phrases in bold, these are the key elements. School bus 1. With signs. 2. Stopped for Loading or UN Loading School Children. 3. With a Flashing red light. 4. And a Stop signal arm (if it has one) Visible from Front or Rear.

> 22454. (a) The driver of any vehicle, upon meeting or overtaking, from either direction, **any school bus equipped with signs** as required in this code, that is **stopped for the purpose of loading or unloading any schoolchildren** and **displays a flashing red light signal** and stop signal arm, as defined in paragraph (4) of subdivision (b) of Section

25257, if equipped with a stop signal arm, visible from front or rear, shall bring the vehicle to a stop immediately before passing the school bus and shall not proceed past the school bus until the flashing red light signal and stop signal arm, if equipped with a stop signal arm, cease operation.

If all the key elements are there then, technically speaking, you violated the law when you passed the bus (but after reading this far in our book you should know that doesn't mean it's the end all and you should just pay the ticket!). If any of those key elements are missing, say the bus was stopped with red flashing lights and a stop signal arm, but there were adults being unloaded and loaded and not school children, then you weren't in violation when you passed the bus. Make sense?

You will find this technique can be used for many different violations. Although this might seem like getting off by a "technicality", the law is very specific for a reason; to protect both sides of an issue!

Another technique to use when dealing with obscure violations is questioning the officer's line of sight to your car or into your car. For tickets relating to seat belts for example, the officer needs to be able to clearly see into your vehicle to judge whether or not your seatbelt was on. If the officer's view was blocked by anything; say a truck in between the two of you, or maybe it was dark and the officer was a couple of lanes away from you when you first saw him, then you can easily show how the officer couldn't have clearly seen into your vehicle. This clearly and simply explains why he mistakenly thought you were not wearing your seatbelt.

Truck Driver Violations
Tickets given to drivers holding a commercial license, like truck drivers, can be very different than those for regular drivers. Tickets for commercial drivers include: driving out of the designated lane; driving over 55 mph; or in some cases over 45 mph or even just 35 mph where there is a reduced truck speed.

Many commercial drivers get a ticket for driving out of lane but there are instances when a driver is permitted to divert from the designated lane that an officer may over look; for example when passing a slower moving vehicle or when it is necessary to continue on your intended route and there is a freeway interchange.

When there is a reduced speed limit of 45 mph or 35 mph sometimes these types of tickets can be treated as you would a ticket for any other type of sign. If the sign was damaged, or blocked in some way which caused it to be hidden from your view, you cannot justly be cited for failing to obey it.

In California, a driver who holds a commercial driver's license cannot just pay the ticket and attend traffic school. Because of this, in cases where the ticket is not completely dismissed, many commercial drivers are able to obtain a reduction to a zero point violation in order to preserve a good driving record since their livelihood depends on it.

Even if you feel as though you have no legal defense to fight your ticket and think there is no hope for keeping a point or more off your driving record since you cannot take traffic school and can't afford to take time off the road to physically go into court, consider using a Trial by Written Declaration. Even if you have a "log book" ticket or an "over weight" ticket and you were clearly in the wrong, you may be surprised that your ticket could potentially be reduced, if not completely dismissed, after using a Trial by Written Declaration.

Options for Handling Traffic Tickets

Now that you have an idea of some of the types of violations you were cited for you need to decide how best to handle the ticket. There are several options and there are downsides to some of these options that you should know about.

Paying the Ticket

Paying the ticket seems easy right. You can just pay the ticket and get rid of the headache right? Not necessarily. If you do pay the ticket you have to worry about points being added to your driving record and an increase to your insurance rates. If you pay for the ticket and attend traffic school you have to waste your valuable time and more of your hard earned money on the cost of attendance and the additional traffic school fees to the court. Fighting the ticket may be a better option for you.

Fighting the Ticket in Court

You can either contact the court or go to court on or before your arraignment date (the date written on the bottom of the ticket near your signature) and request a court trial at which the officer will be present. This is your first opportunity to get your ticket dismissed because if the officer does not show up, your ticket should be dismissed no questions asked. However if the officer does show up you will have to stand up and defend yourself before a judge. If that happens, you may be too nervous or intimated to accurately tell your side of the story and give logical reasons why the ticket should be dismissed. What most people don't know is that they can avoid all this by choosing to fight the ticket using a Trial by Written Declaration. The Trial by Written Declaration, as noted previously, is a written trial submitted to the courts, rather than a trial in which it is necessary for both sides to appear before the judge.

Fighting the Ticket by Trial by Written Declaration

By using a Trial by Written Declaration to fight your ticket you can say everything you had planned to say if you went to court, in writing. You can present your case to the judge in a well thought out manner and never have to step foot in the court room. The option for a Trial by Declaration is generally listed on the back of a ticket or on the courtesy notice you receive from the court. There is no cost to filing a Trial by Declaration with the court on your own although you do need to remember that you will have to pay the bail amount (fine for your ticket) up front and wait for your ticket to be dismissed before you receive that money back from the court. The court will cash your bail check but it will be held in trust pending the outcome of your case. Once the court finds you not guilty, your bail is refunded to you, your case is dismissed and you will have zero points going on your driving record.

Sometimes if the court believes you deserve only a partial dismissal, they can reduce your fine or reduce the ticket to a non-moving violation. In the latter case although you would still have to pay a fine, there won't be any points going on your record so there is no need for you to attend traffic school. Often a ticket reduced to a zero point, non-moving violation, is referred to be "as good as a dismissal". This is especially true for commercial drivers who hold a professional, Class "A" or "B" driver's license who are not permitted to take traffic school.

The beauty of a Trial by Declaration is that even if your ticket is not dismissed fully or reduced to your liking, you can still ask for a New Trial (Trial De Novo) by filing form TR-220 with the court within 20 days of the courts finding you guilty. At the New Trial you will have to appear in court but this still gives you a fresh start and a second opportunity at getting your ticket dismissed. This is considered a completely new trial.

Remember, a Trial by Declaration does not require your appearance in court but, a New Trial (Trial De Novo) will; if it comes to that. Hopefully your ticket will be dismissed and you won't ever have to worry about a new trial. After filing your Trial by Written Declaration with the court, it will take about 30-90 days to hear back from the court. Once the court receives your Trial by Written Declaration, the court notifies the officer by mailing the officer an officer's declaration. An officer's declaration looks like this:

The officer is given a date by which to respond back, and upon arrival of that date, the judge will review the declarations, and then render a decision. It's just as simple as that.

As simple as the Trial by Written Declaration process is, there are still some things you need to know; for example: knowing what to leave out of your Trial by Written Declaration statement can be even more important than knowing what to put into it.

This is covered in the next chapter.

Understanding the Trial by Written Declaration

History of a Trial by Written Declaration

California courts are extremely over crowded. Every time someone comes to court to contest a traffic ticket it takes up valuable court time and money. In 1978, California began a new program in an effort to free up court time while still allowing individuals all the rights afforded them under the law to contest a traffic ticket. California created a "Trial by Written Declaration" as a way to free up the court's time and save the court's money.

A Trial by Written Declaration will allow you to contest your traffic ticket without the need to actually go to court. If the ticket is dismissed, no points will be added to your record and the court will refund your bail in full. If your ticket is not dismissed you can still either request traffic school, if you are eligible, or request a trial in the courtroom to contest your ticket again, a Trial de Novo or Request for New Trial.

This is why contesting a traffic ticket in California with a Trial by Written Declaration is your best option to fight your traffic ticket and keep your driving record clean, saving you money. If you win and your traffic ticket is dismissed, no more points go on your driving record and your bail is fully refunded. If it's not dismissed, no harm is done; you're right back where you started prior to filing a Trial by Written Declaration. Either way you just can't lose!

It just makes sense for anyone who receives a traffic ticket in the state of California to file a Trial by Written Declaration first, prior to choosing to waste their time going to court, or attending traffic school, or just paying the fine.

How to determine if you are eligible for a Trial by Written Declaration

Just about anyone can file a Trial by Written Declaration with a few exceptions.To be eligible to file a Trial by Written Declaration, you need to be over the age of 18. If you were under 18 when you got the ticket most courts require you have your parent or guardian request a Trial by Written Declaration on your behalf. If you were cited for not having a valid driver's license or for driving on a suspended or expired license you generally cannot file a Trial by Written Declaration either.

You must have a traffic ticket that includes a traffic infraction, not a misdemeanor. Speeding tickets, red light camera tickets, lane violation tickets, stop sign tickets and other traffic infractions will all qualify.

However, Drunk Driving, Driving without a valid or on a suspended driver's license, tickets resulting from accidents and other misdemeanors do not qualify.

In addition, your traffic violation must NOT require a mandatory court appearance. If your traffic violation does require a mandatory court appearance, you will need to appear in court on or before the specified date indicated on the ticket and request the judge to set bail and allow you to file a Trial by Written Declaration. If the judge allows you to do this, you can proceed with a Trial by Written Declaration process as discussed previously.

Tickets that are not eligible for a Trial by Written Declaration include: parking tickets, administrative tickets, and other tickets that are not on file with the California Superior Court, like tickets issued by park rangers and U.S. District Courts. Additionally, tickets that are past their due date or that have been referred to a collections agency are no longer eligible for a Trial by Written Declaration.

How to ask the Court for a Trial by Written Declaration

When filing a Trial by Written Declaration, the court must receive your documents no later than the due date of your ticket. We recommend that you get all your documents to the court within 5 days of your specified due date to insure that the court receives everything on time and records it in their system. By doing so, you will avoid any possibility of receiving an FTA, which is a Failure To Appear, for not showing up on your specified court date.

It is not necessary to actually go to the court to file a Trial by Written Declaration. Since the Trial by Written Declaration procedure doesn't require you to actually go to the court house to submit your documents, it's recommend you send all of your documents by certified mail, instead of regular mail. Sending your documents by certified mail guarantees that you have an acknowledgement that the court actually received your documents and the date on which they were received. This is extremely important as, again, you will not actually be appearing in court.

You must file your Trial by Written Declaration documents with the court house indicated at the bottom of ticket or to the address that is indicated on your courtesy notice.

Don't delay in taking care of your traffic ticket! Tickets that have not been taken care of and are past due or have been referred to collections are not eligible for Trial by Written Declaration.

How to File a Trial by Written Declaration

The first step of this process is to obtain the actual Trial by Written Declaration Documents. You can obtain these documents by going to www.TicketBust.com or any Superior Court web site.

A Trial by Written Declaration is a two page document. The first page contains basic information about the court house, bail amount of your ticket and the due date of the ticket and looks like this:

As you can see most of the information required can be found either on your actual ticket or the courtesy notice the court sends you.

If you are including any additional evidence with your Trial by Written Declaration, such as photographs, you need to check the appropriate box at the bottom of the page shown above.

Please note item "B-D" on the Trial by Written Declaration. One major requirement of a Trial by Written Declaration is that you post your bail with the court when filing a Trial by Written Declaration. This is a court requirement. Since you will not be going to court to contest your traffic ticket, the court requires you to post your bail in order for it to consider your Trial by Written Declaration.

When the court receives your documents, they will cash your bail check and put it in the court's client trust account. If your ticket is dismissed, your bail will be refunded to you in the form of a court check. If your ticket is not dismissed they will convert your bail to the fine for the ticket and close your case.

The second page of the Trial by Written Declaration is the "Statement of Facts" and looks like this:

At the top of the page you must put your full legal name and your case or citation number. After that you will indicate your mailing address. This is the address that you would like the court to send any communications to, including your decision notice. This address does NOT have to be the same as the address on your driver's license; however it should be an address at which the mail is checked on a regular basis.

Next comes your actual Statement of Facts. This is where you will present your case to the court. Keep in mind that there is only a small space here but you can attach additional pages as necessary to fully explain your case properly. You should make sure that you present your case in a clear and concise manner. Take the time to make your points, but do not run on excessively as the court will lose interest.

If you do need to attach additional pages, be sure to put your name and case or citation number at the top of each page and the page number at the bottom of each page.

What to Include in a Trial by Written Declaration and What Not to Include

As already noted, any Trial by Written Declaration will include a Statement of Facts. Here you should begin by briefly summarizing what exactly you were cited for and include all relevant facts, including anything important about the driving conditions that day such as the weather and the traffic. You can tell your side of the story and also bring up any possible defenses. You must include discussion of any photographs, diagrams, or witness statements you plan to include with the Trial by Declaration documents (photos, diagrams, and witness statements can be very helpful to your case).

If you were cited for more than one thing on the same ticket, remember to include a discussion about all of them in the same declaration document. If you were cited for more than one violation but they are listed on different tickets then you will need to use a separate Trial by Declaration for each ticket.

Remember you don't have to include every single detail! Avoid putting in details which will have a negative impact. For example, if you were cited for traveling too fast on a city street you would probably want to mention that there were NO pedestrians or parks nearby, but if there WERE pedestrians and a park nearby you are better off NOT mentioning it. If you were cited for speeding on a freeway, but you were being passed by other vehicles you definitely want to mention this to show how much more reasonable your speed was than other motorists around you. However if you were the one passing all the other cars, it's probably best not to bring that up. If there was some sort of emergency situation that explains why you did what you did resulting in the ticket, you will have to really consider just how significant this "emergency" was. On one hand a judge may sympathize with you, however, you are also admitting guilt at this point, so if it is something that was not truly an emergency, like needing to find a restroom really badly, that excuse is probably not going to be very effective in getting your ticket dismissed.

At all costs please avoid bad mouthing the officer who pulled you over, (no matter how angry you may be about getting a ticket) this will not help gain a judges sympathy and in fact may irritate the judge. If you feel strongly that the officer's behavior was inappropriate during the course of your interaction though, then you do have the right to file a complaint with the Police Department through which the officer is employed. The Judicial Officer reviewing your Trial by Written Declaration statement is not interested in hearing about the officer's bad manners nor is he interested in unnecessary details. Be complete in your explanation and reasons, but also be succinct.

The average time a Judicial Officer spends reviewing a Trial by Declaration statement is 5–10 minutes. That's why you need to present your Trial by Declaration statement in a neat and organized fashion and include only those facts and details which are truly relevant. Conclude your declaration statement by respectfully requesting that the court dismiss the ticket in its entirety.

At www.TicketBust.com we have many years of experience writing Trial by Declaration statements and we know how to document the facts of your case in ways that will maximize your chances at getting out of your ticket. The following section will show some excerpts of our work. Please be aware these are just small portions of a full declaration statement and your Trial by Written Declaration statement can be simple or more complex.

Sample Trial by Written Declaration Statements

The following Trial by Declaration statement was prepared for our client out of Las Vegas, NV who had a speeding ticket with the Pittsburg courthouse due on 8/6/10. We prepared and filed a Trial by Declaration for this client on 7/23/10 and the ticket was dismissed 1/21/11. The following is a small portion of her statement:

> "On the day I was issued the citation at issue in this case, I was driving west on Highway 4 amongst a moderate amount of traffic... The officer claims to have estimated my speed at 80 mph and has indicated that he relied on a radar instrument however I had my cruise control set to the speed limit and was traveling at the same pace as traffic around me. There was no way I could have been traveling at 80 mph...Here my vehicle was not the only vehicle within the officer's range... I believe that the officer actually clocked another car and attributed their speed to mine. The common problem with radar units, even the modern models, is that the read is generally inaccurate because the radar beams are not tight and narrow... In this case, I was going along with the flow of traffic, traveling with vehicles around me and thus the officer had no clear line to my vehicle. Without a clear line of sight to my vehicle, he could not have received a perfect read of my speed..."

Her statement also included a discussion of calibration requirements of the officer's radar, training requirements for the officer's use of radar, and the effect the lack of a clear line of sight would have on the officer's determination of her speed. Our case consultants also discovered a flaw on the ticket itself and included a discussion on this as well.

The following Trial by Declaration statement was prepared for our client out of San Bruno, CA who had a red light camera ticket with the San Mateo courthouse due on 12/20/10. We prepared and filed a Trial by Declaration for this client on 12/09/10 and the ticket was dismissed 1/31/11. The following is a small portion of his statement:

> "In this matter, there is no officer to testify in this case, but rather the prosecution is relying on an automated enforcement device – a red-light camera... While these red-

light camera systems are legal in California pursuant to VC§21455.5, if the People wish to convict me of violating a signal, it is their duty pursuant to VC§ 21455.5(c)(2)(C) to first establish that the signal was installed and operating according to the law... Should the People fail to establish that this foundational requirement is met then respectfully the Court cannot find me guilty of this infraction for the People will have failed to meet their burden of proof... The primary purpose for these red light cameras is supposed to be for the public safety and not a revenue generator... When I made a right turn at the intersection (where I saw no sign prohibiting a turn on red) I could not have possibly constituted a safety hazard to me or to others... At no time during the turning movement was there a car close enough to constitute a hazard..."

His Trial by Declaration statement included discussions on the Notice To Appear - Mandatory Language/Data Fields due to the fact a case consultant found a flaw on his ticket, and also discussed requirements of Documentation of 30-Day Grace Period, Public Announcement, Yellow Light Change Interval Documentation, Warning Signs at Camera-Equipped Intersections, Confidentiality, and Clear Photographic Evidence.

This next Trial by Written Declaration statement was prepared for our client out of Chula Vista, CA who had a red light ticket issued by a motorcycle officer. The ticket was due with the Chula Vista courthouse on 1/26/11. We prepared and filed a Trial by Declaration for this client on 1/10/11 and the ticket was dismissed 3/14/11.

"In this matter, I am being accused of violating California Vehicle Code Section 21453... On the day I was issued the citation at issue in this case, I was traveling East on Camino De La Plaza amongst light traffic. The weather was clear at the time and I was driving at a speed which was reasonable and prudent, having due regard for weather, visibility, traffic, and the surface and width of the roadway... While traveling,

I approached a traffic controlled intersection at Camino De La Plaza and the Interstate 5 on ramp and prepared to turn right. At this time, I neared the limit line and the light was red so I did not proceed with the right hand turn without first ensuring it was clear for me to turn. The officer who issued me the citation was not directly to the side of the intersection, lined up with the limit line... without a clear view of the limit line the officer could not have seen whether my car stopped at the limit line..."

His Trial by Declaration statement included discussion on the officer's lack of a clear line of sight and also discussion on the flaw a case consultant found on his ticket.

This Trial by Declaration statement was prepared for a client out of Oak Park, CA who had an uncommon ticket for "disobeying a sign" by speeding. This ticket was due to the Simi Valley courthouse by 1/26/11. We prepared and filed a Trial by Declaration for this client on 1/24/11 and the ticket was dismissed 5/9/11.

"In this matter , I am being accused of violating California Vehicle Code Section 38300...California Vehicle Code section 38300 reads: "It is unlawful for the driver of any vehicle to disobey any sign... The officer did not make clear that there was any particular sign which I disobeyed, however I observed that on the citation it is indicated that my approximate speed was 63 mph and that the posted speed was 45 mph, so perhaps the officer is alleging I did not obey a posted speed sign... However the speed limit sign in question must have been missed by me as when I revisited the stretch of Kanan (between the point where I entered onto it and the point at which I was pulled over), I observed certain speed limit signs to be posted near trees in heavily shaded areas on the far right side of the road, where such a sign could easily be missed by a passing motorist such as myself...

His Trial by Written Declaration statement also included discussion on the requirements for the officer's evidence of laser to be considered and how the officer's lack of a clear line of sight to his vehicle could have affected the officer's read of his speed.

This next Trial by Written Declaration statement was prepared for our client out of Coachella, CA who had an unsafe lane change ticket due to the Long Beach courthouse on 3/28/11. We prepared and filed a Trial by Declaration for this client on 3/17/11 and the ticket was dismissed 5/24/11.

> "In this matter I am being accused of violating California Vehicle Code Section 21658 (a). On the day I was issued the citation at issue in this case, I was traveling west on Anaheim amongst moderately light traffic. The weather was clear and I was driving at a speed which was reasonable and prudent, having due regard for weather, visibility, traffic, and the surface and width of the roadway...I was traveling in the right lane and then made a seemingly safe lane change over to the left lane because the lane I was in was coming to an end. I did not cut off any other vehicle and out of habit I used my turn signal if there is any car near enough that could be affected. This occasion was no different... The officer could not have accurately judged whether any infraction was committed or not without a clear line of sight..."

His complete statement included some lengthy discussion which discounted the officer's observations of his vehicle based on a lack of a clear line of sight.

Using our tips and tricks we don't think you'll lose but if your ticket does not get dismissed, do not worry, all is not lost! In the next section we'll explain what your options are if your ticket is not dismissed and what the next step is if you are found guilty on the Trial by Written Declaration.

Understanding the New Trial Process

After filing your Trial by Written Declaration with the court, it takes the court about 30-90 days to actually render a decision and then mail that notice of decision to you. If you open the notice and it says you were found not guilty then you will receive a refund of your bail money in about 60 days and there will be no point going on your record. If you were found guilty, your next step would be to request a New Trial or a Trial De Novo which would give you a second opportunity to contest the ticket for a dismissal.

The court will generally include the paperwork necessary to do this but if not you can obtain these documents by going to www.TicketBust.com or any Superior Court web site. The document looks like this:

TR-220

NAME OF COURT:
STREET ADDRESS:
MAILING ADDRESS:
CITY AND ZIP CODE:
BRANCH NAME:

PEOPLE OF THE STATE OF CALIFORNIA
vs.
DEFENDANT:

REQUEST FOR NEW TRIAL (TRIAL DE NOVO)
(Trial by Written Declaration—Vehicle Code, § 40902)

CITATION NUMBER:

CASE NUMBER:

1. The clerk mailed the court's *Decision and Notice of Decision* (form TR-215) in my trial by written declaration to me on *(date)*:

2. I am submitting this request to the court within 20 days of the date in item 1. *(The court must receive this request within 20 days of the date in item 1.)*

3. I am dissatisfied with the court's decision. I request a new trial (trial de novo) for the following violations *(specify)*:

Date:

(TYPE OR PRINT NAME) (SIGNATURE)

IF YOU WISH TO REQUEST A NEW TRIAL, YOU MUST SUBMIT A *REQUEST FOR NEW TRIAL (TRIAL DE NOVO)* WITHIN 20 DAYS OF THE DATE STATED IN THE CLERK'S CERTIFICATE OF MAILING *(see item 1 above)*.

Form Adopted by the
Judicial Council of California
TR-220 New January 1, 1999

REQUEST FOR NEW TRIAL (TRIAL DE NOVO)
(Trial by Written Declaration—Traffic)

Vehicle Code, § 40902

Please note the top portion of the document contains space for basic information about the court house, your legal name, your citation number. On Line 1–3 you will need to put the date of the court's decision (which you will find on the bottom on the decision notice mailed to you), the date you are submitting the documents on, and space to write the violations you were cited for that you plan to contest at the New Trial. You will also need to print your name, sign and date the bottom of the document in the spaces provided before sending it off to the court. As we mentioned before, any correspondence mailed to the court should be sent by at least Certified Mail so you have tracking and proof of receipt. This is especially important because in order to be eligible for a New Trial you must request one within 20 days of the court finding you guilty on the Trial by Written Declaration. If you get the forms signed, filled out, and filed with the court on time then you will be granted a New Trial and the court will mail a notice to you indicating the date you have to appear. If you would like to change or postpone your court date you will need to contact the court as soon as possible, if the request is made when there is less than 14 days prior to your court date it is unlikely that the court will be able to honor your request. If you decide not to go to the New Trial after all then call the court to cancel, but be aware if you do not proceed with the New Trial the court's decision on the Trial by Declaration will stand. The officer will also be notified of the court date so he or she may choose to appear. After you have your court date the next step is to prepare anything you might want to take with you to court .

Preparing for the New Trial

It is helpful to know what the officer put in the Officer's Declaration. If you are able to view the officer's declaration prior to your court date you can review it for any useful information, and weaknesses, inconsistencies or provable falsehoods to be used at trial. If you are at court the day of your trial and still don't have a copy of the officer's declaration you can (before it's your turn in front of the judge) make an inquiry for it at the traffic clerk window or approach the bailiff for direction on where to obtain it. The majority of courts will allow you to see this (the Officer's Declaration) prior to the conclusion of the New Trial, however a few courts may try and tell you no, that you have to wait until the New Trial is concluded. Unfortunately, if this is the case, you may need to ask to speak with a court supervisor or go in person to the court and ask to speak with someone who has some authority. It may help to ask where the court has this rule (not allowing you to see something that is a matter of public record until after the New Trial is concluded) in writing for you to see, as it is likely they do not. If you are told by the court that you will have to pay a copy fee per page for your own copy of the Officer's Declaration you would need to do this or you can ask to view it for free in person at the courthouse (if you don't want your own copy).

If at any point you are told by the court that the officer failed to respond to your Trial by Written Declaration, when you go to court and it is your turn in front of the judge, you can state something to this effect: "The court system allowed my trial to be conducted by a Trial by Written Declaration. The officer chose not to respond to the court. The officer was the state's only witness in this case against me and because the state's only witness chose not to respond there was no evidence offered to disprove my innocence. The burden of proof in this case is beyond a reasonable doubt and that burden is incumbent upon the state. In this case I am innocent until proven guilty and the state offered no evidence to disprove my innocence. For reason of lack of prosecution, I respectfully ask this court to dismiss my case".

Something else that can be helpful is obtaining a copy of the engineering and traffic survey (if a speeding ticket), the officer's notes, or similar documents relevant to your case before the trial. These types of things can be requested prior to trial, sometimes by just making a simple phone call to the courthouse, city clerk, police department where the officer is employed, or it can be done through a more formal process called discovery.

You should also start thinking about whether you have any witnesses you can bring along with you to court to testify on your behalf. If you have photos, diagrams, etc. that you think support your case make copies and have them enlarged to take with you to court.

You can take notes with you to the trial and if you kept a copy of your Trial by Written Declaration you can refer to this too, to help you remember what you want to say in court. Since this is a new trial you can change any of the information you present in court and add any new facts you wish to. Now that you have an idea what types of things you should bring to court, you can start to think about what to expect when you actually arrive at court.

Appearing for the New Trial

You will know when and where to appear in court by the notice the court mailed to you in response to your request for a New Trial. Plan to arrive early so you can find parking and your court room. You don't want to be late when your name is called to go in front of the judge. You should dress nicely and show up to court at least 30 minutes prior to your trial time.

If you are called up and the officer is not there, you may request that the case against you be dismissed due to lack of prosecution (that is of course if the court doesn't automatically dismiss your case on its own motion). If needed, you can refer the court to Penal Code Section 1385 which says "1385. (a) The judge or magistrate may, either of his or her own motion or upon the application of the prosecuting attorney, and in furtherance of justice, order an action to be dismissed." If the officer is there, the officer will generally be called to testify first which gives you a chance to listen to the officer's side of the story and afterwards you will have a chance to explain your side and bring up any defenses and evidence you have.

Explain your version of what happened in a clear, honest and convincing manner and avoid "iffy" type words like, "possibly", "maybe", "if" or other similar words. Feel free to ask the judge questions, speak politely and address the judge as "your honor". Be confident in your presentation and positive, polite, and direct with the court.

Asking Questions

Remember you can ask the officer any questions you want; you can use any notes you made so you don't have to have them memorized. If you have a copy of the officer's notes there may be a difference or inconsistency in what the officer says and what's written in his or her notes on the ticket (same goes for what is written on the officer's declaration) that you can bring up to discredit the officer's testimony. You may find it helpful to stick to questions that require a "yes" or "no" answer (or a brief, factual response rather than questions that give the officer a chance to state his opinion), or asking questions such as these:

Speeding Violations

- How did the officer measure your speed?
- Was it a visual estimation, a mechanical device (laser or radar) or both?

- If laser or radar was used, how does the officer know it was working?

- Were there tests performed, are there repair/test logs kept by the police department?

- When was the officer trained and who trained him? Visual estimations, laser and radar all require training. This training must be offered by someone qualified to train and this training must have taken place prior to the issuance of the speeding ticket in question.

Failure To Obey Sign Violations

Was there notice of the sign in question? How you could you be found guilty of violating a sign unless the officer testified that you passed a visible sign in that area?

You of course could respond by stating any reasons or presenting any evidence showing the sign was not there or was not visible.

In General

The purpose in questioning the officer is to demonstrate that there is reasonable doubt that you are guilty.

For example, to try and have the officer admit that you did not violate every element of the law or that he was not in a position to see your vehicle clearly or that he misinterpreted the event leading up to the citation.

Asking for Reductions

If you find yourself facing a guilty verdict, there are some alternatives to ask for such as a reduction. Remember, a reduction to a zero point or non-moving violation does not necessarily mean you will be getting any money refunded to from the court from the fine you paid for the ticket. It does however mean that no point would be going on your driving record and since there would be no point to affect your driving record, you would not need to pay the extra money or waste your time attending traffic school.

Speeding Tickets (and for those with a Commercial Driver's License)
Ask for the ticket to be lowered to a zero point violation, such as a
coasting infraction (21710 (VC) "Coasting in Neutral on
Downgrade Prohibited") so it does not affect your driving
privilege. This is in lieu of the court entering a finding of guilty as
to the California Vehicle Code section you were originally cited for.

Red light, stop sign, or other ticket involving a sign or signal
Ask for the ticket to be lowered to a zero point violation, such as
38300 (VC) "Unlawful to Disobey Specified Sign, Signal, or Traffic
Control Device" so it does not affect your driving privilege. This is
in lieu of the court entering a finding of guilty as to the California
Vehicle Code section you were originally cited for.

Other tickets
If this is not a speeding, red light ticket or a type of ticket involving
a sign, you could ask that the ticket be amended to add a violation
of the local Municipal Code that is not a moving violation so it
does not affect your driving privilege. This is in lieu of the court
entering a finding of guilty as to the California Vehicle Code
section you were originally cited for.

Asking for Traffic School

If you are not able to get a dismissal or a reduction then your last
resort would be to ask for traffic school. According to Vehicle Code
section 42005 and pertaining to *People v. Enochs* (1976) 62
Cal.App.3d Supp. 42 and *People v. Wozniak* (1987) 197 Cal.App.3d
Supp. 43 you can still request to attend traffic school even after
you have been found guilty of the alleged violation, if you were
eligible for traffic school prior to being found guilty.

The trial judge has the power to order you to attend traffic school if
the trial judge believes that your circumstances indicate that you
would benefit from attending school, such attendance should be
authorized.

The question of such imposition of traffic school should not be
affected by the order in which plea, explanation and request (for

school) are presented as to decide on you entitlement to traffic school on the basis of the order of presentation rather than the facts of the case is capricious and arbitrary.

You may politely request traffic school stating a reason why it would benefit you.

The grant of traffic school is at the sole discretion of the judge.

Final Decision

If you were found not guilty you can expect to receive a refund of your bail money in about 60 days and since your case was dismissed you will not have to worry about any points going on your record. If you were found guilty and you posted bail as you were supposed to along with the Trial by Declaration then you should not owe any additional fees to the court. If the court imposed any additional fees such as Traffic School fees though you will have to pay those and upon completion of Traffic School the DMV would be notified of the court authorized dismissal by traffic school. If you were still found guilty but the ticket was reduced the court will let you know if you are owed any sort of refund.

Although this is considered the final decision on your case, you could decide to appeal it. A proper appeal of a traffic court decision would be because some sort of prejudicial error was made during your trial (i.e. the judge applied the wrong law and you were found guilty based on the use of the wrong law) as opposed to appealing the decision just because you aren't happy with it. Appeals are not the same as a new trial, the appellate court will not consider new evidence and will only review the decision made on your case to see if a legal error was made. Appeals are more involved than a Trial by Written Declaration or Trial De Novo and although you could do it on your own most people have a lawyer represent them for this. If needed, information on appeal procedures and the necessary forms can be found on the Judicial Council of California website at www.courtinfo.ca.gov.

Finally (A Better Way)

While it is true that anyone can do a Trial by Written Declaration on their own, we don't advise it unless you know exactly what to say and more importantly what not to say. This takes time and years of experience fine tuning statements and declarations to be effective. As an example, let's say a pipe broke in your kitchen sink. You could certainly run down to your local hardware store and purchase the necessary parts and try to fix the pipe yourself or you can call an expert, a plumber, who has fixed thousands of sinks and knows exactly how best to fix that pipe so that it will not break again in the future. The same thing holds true with a preparing a Trial By Written Declaration. If you have never prepared one before, or even if you have prepared a few, you most likely do not know what to say and way not to say. You do not have the experience of knowing what the courts are looking for. It's always best to go to an expert like TicketBust.com and let us prepare the documents properly for you in order to maximize your chances of getting your ticket dismissed.

Preparing a truly effective and quality Trial by Written Declaration statement is a learned art which is why this book was created, to show you there is a better way to contest a traffic ticket. Drive safely out there but the next time you do get pulled over remember that TicketBust.com is on your side. As you are signing that ticket and are thinking to yourself, "what am I going to do about this", don't fall prey to rolling over and paying that ticket! Don't get duped into just showing up in court unprepared. Remember there IS a better way to contest that traffic ticket. Have confidence cause with our book you've got the tips, tricks, and must knows you need to successfully contest that ticket!

50 Traffic Ticket Tips

Getting pulled over for a traffic ticket can be a traumatic experience. What do you do when you get pulled over? What should you say to the officer? More importantly, what should you not say when getting pulled over? Based on discussions with clients and our years of experience, TicketBust.com has put together a list of things to do and things to avoid doing.

We provide these tips to all our clients. In fact, we have produced a "Glove Box Folder" that includes all our traffic ticket tips right on the folder. Keep this folder in your car as an easy reminder and also place a copy of your insurance and registration inside the folder. You can refer to this folder any time you get pulled over by an officer.

Anyone that signs up for our service at www.TicketBust.com receives our "Glove Box Folder" mailed to them automatically. We have also provided you a list of our 50 Traffic Ticket Tips below:

Tips for when you are pulled over by an officer

1. Stay Calm
2. Pull over safely and quickly to the right
3. Signal when pulling over
4. Pull far enough over so the officer can stand w/out getting hit
5. Remain in your vehicle, unless the officer instructs you to get out
6. Ask for identification if the officer is not uniformed or you're uncertain
7. Roll down the driver's side window all the way
8. Turn off your engine
9. Lock your doors
10. Place the car keys on the dash

11. If it's dark out, make the officer more comfortable by turning on the dome light
12. Keep both hands on the steering wheel
13. Leave your seatbelt on
14. Be courteous - this may result in a reduced penalty or warning
15. Ask permission before reaching for items
16. Tell the officer what you are reaching for and where it is
17. Follow the officer's instructions
18. Remember you have the right to remain silent
19. Keep a car wallet w/insurance, registration & copy of license
20. Keep pad & pen in car - for writing down details of the stop
21. Keep a camera in car - go back asap to take pics of the area where you were stopped
22. If you work or live close to the County Seat and would prefer to have your case moved there, you have the right to request it
23. Keep all your answers brief and non-incriminating
24. When leaving, pull out safely and use your signal
25. If you have passengers in the car, ask them to remain silent unless spoken to first by the officer.
26. If the officer asks: "Do you know why I pulled you over?" The safest answer you can give is: "No, I was driving safely."

What not to do when you get pulled over by an officer

27. DON'T admit guilt to any particular speed (or anything for that matter)!
28. Officer not required to show speed gun, DON'T argue if answers no, make a note later
29. DON'T take pics, do or say anything memorable in front of the officer

30. DON'T linger and write down notes for more than a second or two after a traffic stop
31. DON'T let the officer know you plan to fight the ticket
32. DON'T make any sudden movements
33. DON'T offer any info. Always wait for the officer to ask
34. If the officer says "no" to your request to have your ticket transferred to the County Seat? DON'T argue, just write "county seat requested" next to your signature.

Tips for when you are caught on camera

35. Go back and time the yellow light with a stopwatch
36. Check if any camera enforcement warning signs were posted and where.
37. Note if you made any turns or went straight (same true for a stop sign or non camera red light)

Tips for when you get a speeding ticket

38. If you're pulled over for speeding, take note of how fast the officer says you were going.
39. If the officer asks "How fast were you going?" The ONLY answer is: "A safe and reasonable speed."
40. Make note of the location, road conditions, traffic, and weather.
41. Keep track of any and all statements that the officer makes; but take no more than a few seconds to jot them down when officer goes back to his car.
42. Make note if there were or are any pedestrians, schools, or parks nearby.
43. Note where officer was when you first saw him.
44. If the officer is carrying a radar or lidar speed gun and the officer shows it to you, don't make any comments about it, but do try to note the manufacturer and model of the device.

45. If the officer did not use a radar/lidar device, note how long the officer was following you.

Tips for when you get a stop sign ticket or red light ticket

46. Note where in relation to the limit line both you and the officer were when the light turned red
47. Take pictures from the officer's view and note any obstructions of both the limit line and the stop sign
48. If asked why you didn't stop for a stop sign a safe answer is: "you didn't proceed until safe"
49. If there is a posted sign take pictures of the sign and anything blocking it - note anything that could have prevented you from seeing it

What to do after you get a ticket

50. Remember that TicketBust.com is on your side!
   - Go to our web site at www.TicketBust.com and select the "To Bust My Ticket Now" option or "Start Right Now." Just fill out the information and we will do the rest.
   - Remember if you have a mobile phone you can download our iTicketBust App and take a picture of your ticket and submit it via your mobile device. Go to http://www.TicketBust.com/app-page.html

Traffic Ticket Excuses

The following humorous stories about speeding ticket excuses that law enforcement has heard (or had to endure) in the line of duty. In this article, Greg Williams, a California Highway Patrol officer claims to have heard them all and shares his experiences with speeding drivers' excuses. This proves there is not much a person will not say to get out of a ticket. Williams said there have been some good ones over the years, including the following:

1.   In the mid-80s, Williams pulled over a Corvette on I-5 that had been doing 125 mph. The driver's speeding ticket excuse..."I couldn't be going that fast. My speedometer only goes to 85 mph."

2.   A common speeding ticket excuse involves either a pregnant wife or a sick relative. Williams said he once pulled over a man for speeding and the man's pregnant wife was in the passenger seat. He said he was speeding because he needed to get her to the hospital. "She was showing pretty good, but she wasn't that far along," Williams said. Williams told the driver he would follow him to the hospital. The man drove as far as Kern Medical Center's parking lot before getting out of his car, walking up to Williams' cruiser and saying, "I lied."

3.   Williams once stopped an older couple on Highway 99 near Taft Highway driving 20 miles over the speed limit. He said it was apparent the wife was angry at the husband, who was driving. Williams asked where they were headed and the husband replied that they were going to his son's place in Ventura. Where had they started? West L.A. "When did you notice the ocean wasn't on your left side?" Williams asked. Apparently, the wife had been trying to get her husband to turn around for at least the past half hour, but he refused. Williams gave them directions, but he's not sure it helped. "Last I saw they were still northbound on 99 going through Bakersfield." As far as we can see this speeding ticket excuse worked!

4.   An officer responded to a fender bender and asked the driver at fault what happened. The driver asked the officer if he wanted the truth or the story he made up. At this point, the officer should have known there'd be a story to tell here. The officer asked for the truth. The driver said he had been picking his nose and reached

for a tissue. When he looked up it was too late to avoid the fender bender. The made up story? He was going to tell the officer he was switching radio stations when the crash happened.

Traffic Ticket Talk Series

About TicketTalk

In an attempt to reach as many people as possible, In 2010 TicketBust.com began running a web series (webisode) on YouTube entitled TicketTalk. With our TicketTalk series we have embarked on an educational track to provide viewers relevant traffic ticket information, current news related to traffic ticket infractions, what you should know about when you receive a traffic ticket.

To get an idea of the focus and content provided in our TicketTalk Webisode series, below is a short synopsis of the show:

At TicketTalk we will discuss various Traffic Ticket topics providing you with relevant information about what to do when you receive a traffic ticket and how to fight and contest a Traffic Ticket. We will also update you on changes you should be aware of related to driving safely and keep from getting Traffic Ticket. Topics will include how a Trial by Written Declaration works and how it is filed. We will also be providing relevant California Traffic Ticket information about Red Light Photo/Camera Tickets, Speeding Tickets, Lane Change Tickets and other traffic infractions. Keep in mind that TicketBust.com can help you contest that speeding ticket, red light ticket, red light camera ticket or other traffic infraction in the state of California.

Transcripts of our Traffic TicketTalk Webisodes

We know that in this day and age just the printed word is not enough, video helps. We don't want you to just read this book, we want to engage you to use all the tools and resources we have included. So take your time and enjoy our TicketTalk Webisode series. We have included a print summary of each webisode currently available through August 2011 along with links to the actual video. As we release more webisodes you can find them on our web site at http://www.TicketBust.com/traffic-ticket-defense/index.html or on YouTube by going to our channel at TicketBust_CA.

Webisode #1 – Introduction to TicketTalk
http://www.youtube.com/watch?v=fvrOrJahlHY&feature=player_embedded

Here's a fact for you - California issues over 16 million traffic violations every year and one out of every six drivers will get a speeding ticket in a year. What can you do when you receive a traffic ticket? Well, you're not alone; many people are confused and really don't know what to do.

They either just pay the ticket or request traffic school, and some may even go to court when they don't need to.

Fortunately there are other options in California for all drivers who receive traffic tickets. And it doesn't matter if they live in California or outside the state, the only requirement is that it's a California traffic ticket.

So, before you waste your time and just pay the ticket or go to traffic school, you should consider filing a Trial by Written Declaration. A Trial by Written Declaration will allow you to contest your traffic ticket without the need of court to contest your ticket. If the ticket is dismissed, you will have no points on your record and the court will refund your bail.

Now the beauty of a trial by written declaration is that if your ticket is not dismissed you can still either request traffic school, if you are eligible, or request an in-court trial to contest your ticket again, this is known as a Trial de Novo or request for New Trial.

And this is why contesting a traffic ticket in the state California with a Trial by Written Declaration is your best option to fight your traffic ticket and keep your driving record clean, which saves you money and reduces your insurance cost. If your traffic ticket is dismissed you win, no points on your record and your bail is refunded. if it's not dismissed, no harm done; you're right back where you started prior to filing a Trial by Written Declaration.

My advice to anyone who receives a traffic ticket in the state of California is to file a Trial by Written Declaration first, prior to electing traffic school, going to court, or just paying the fine.

Webisode #2 – What To Do If You Get an LA Camera Ticket: Don't Ignore That Ticket
http://www.youtube.com/watch?v=v09w63_fiew&feature=player_embedded

Word has gotten around, after the recent LA Times article about camera tickets, that LA courts don't report a person to the DMV if they fail to pay a Red Light Camera Ticket. This has left many people thinking that this is a green light to ignore those red light tickets.

Well, my advice to you is DON'T IGNORE THAT TICKET.

You see, a Red Light Camera Ticket is sent to the registered owner of a vehicle and if the registered owner doesn't pay, the court sends another notice stating an additional $300 is owed if not paid within 10 days. After that the registered owner's name is sent to collections.

If you don't pay in LA County your license might not be suspended, but you can bet a collections agency will be harassing you and this could have a major negative impact on your credit.

Also keep in mind that the court's policy seems to be specific as to the registered owner's name that appears on the ticket so the court may not apply the same policy if you are not the registered owner even if your name is on the ticket. If the court chooses not to apply their policy to you then your license can be suspended.

LA Superior Court may be one of the only counties, if not the only county, having this policy. Since it is a court policy that the court has elected to make, and they were not forced to make, it could change at any time. So in choosing to ignore the ticket and let it go to collections, you are taking a big risk because that policy could change without you knowing.

Conclusion – DON'T IGNORE THAT TICKET, it will cost you more in the long run.

Webisode #3 – Qualifications for a Trial by Written Declaration
http://www.youtube.com/watch?v=RqJUD57ddsw&feature=player_embedded

Last week we introduced you to the idea that traffic tickets can be fought, contested and dismissed using a California Trial by Written Declaration. This week we are going to review some of the qualifications for a Trial by Written Declaration and who can file a Trial by Written Declaration.

To review, A Trial by Written Declaration is a way to contest a Traffic Ticket without going to court.

To be eligible to file a Trial by Written Declaration, you need to be over the age of 18 and have a valid driver's license.

You must have a traffic ticket that includes only a traffic infraction, not a misdemeanor. Speeding tickets, red light camera tickets, lane violation tickets, stop sign ticket and other traffic infractions all will qualify. However, drunk driving, driving without a valid or on a suspended driver's license, tickets involving accidents and other misdemeanors do not qualify.

In addition, your traffic violation must NOT require a mandatory court appearance. If your traffic violation requires a mandatory court appearance, you will need to appear in court on or before the specified date indicated on the ticket and request the judge to set bail and allow you to file a Trial by Written Declaration. If the judge allows this, great then you're good to go and can proceed with a Trial by Written Declaration as normal.

Other tickets that are not eligible for a Trial by Written Declaration include, parking tickets, administrative tickets, and other tickets that are not on file with the California Superior Court, like tickets issued by park rangers and U.S. District Courts

You can obtain the actual Trial by Written Declaration Documents by going to www.TicketBust.com or any superior court web site.

Webisode #4 – Tips on Routine Traffic Stops
http://www.youtube.com/watch?v=pPlxCRFlkoU&feature=player_embedded

Getting a traffic ticket doesn't have to be a traumatic experience. In this week's webisode of Ticket Talk you'll get a few tips on how best to handle yourself during a routine traffic stop.

First up, remember, it's the law to pull over to the right.

When you see the flashing lights behind you, pull over to the right as safely and quickly as you can.

Many people make the mistake of pulling to the left if they are already in the left lane and they end up getting a ticket for that as well.

You need to find a place safe to stop, but try to avoid traveling for a long distance, you DON'T want the officer to think you're trying to get away and, you DON'T want to get a ticket for failing to yield.

Alright, the next few tips are all about making the officer feel comfortable. The more comfortable the officer is and the more smoothly the traffic stop goes, the more likely the officer might let you off with just a warning!

After you pull over you'll want to:

- Remain in your car and roll down your window
- You should turn off the engine and place the keys on the dash
- And you'll want to place both your hands on the wheel

Now once the officer walks up to your window you'll want to:

- Be courteous and follow the officer's instructions
- Keep your answers brief
- And always ask permission before reaching for any items. Make sure the officer knows what item you're reaching for and where it's located, that way he doesn't think you're reaching for a weapon

It's also a good idea to keep a notepad, pen, and camera in your glove box. Before you leave the scene and while the officer is busy writing up the ticket, you can jot down a few quick notes about the traffic and weather and any comments the officer made. This information will be useful later if you decide to fight your ticket.

You can go back later and take photos of the area and of any posted signs, you don't want to linger at the scene while the officer is there as this is a red flag you plan to fight the ticket.

Remember these simple tips for a much more pleasant ticketing experience!

Webisode #5 – Where and When To File A Trial by Written Declaration
http://www.youtube.com/watch?v=ArcZ5igTY7Y&feature=player_embedded

For the last couple of weeks we've been discussing how to fight a traffic ticket and get it dismissed by using a California Trial By Written Declaration and this is the third part in that discussion series. This week we will discuss who can file a Trial by Written Declaration along with where and when to file.

In California anyone over the age of 18 with a valid driver's license may contest a traffic ticket using a Trial by Written Declaration. You don't have to have a California Driver's License or live in the state of California. The only requirement is that the ticket is issued in the state of California. Obviously, if you live out of state, filing a Trial by Written Declaration is the most convenient way to fight a traffic ticket since you will not have to appear in court.

When filing a Trial by Written Declaration, the court must receive your documents no later than the due date of your ticket. We recommend that you get all your documents to the court within 5 days of your specified due date to insure that the court receives everything on time and records it in their system. This way you will avoid receiving an FTA, which is a failure to appear, for not showing up on your specified court date.

It is not necessary to actually go to the court to file a Trial by Written Declaration. Since you will not be going to the court house to submit your documents, we always recommend you send them by certified mail, not regular mail. This way you have an acknowledgement that the court actually received your documents and the date that they received the documents. Again, this is extremely important as you will not actually be appearing in court.

You must file your Trial by Declaration documents with the court house indicated at the bottom of ticket or the address that is indicated on your courtesy notice.

Don't delay in taking care of your traffic ticket! Tickets that have not been taken care of and are past due or have been referred to collections are not eligible for Trial by Written Declaration.

Remember you can obtain the actual Trial by Written Declaration Documents by going to www.TicketBust.com or any superior court web site.

Webisode #6 – Does an Officer Have To Show the Radar Gun?
http://www.youtube.com/watch?v=Aj-YlyRA1mw&feature=player_embedded

Last week we gave you some tips to remember for when you get pulled over, and this webisode you'll get a few more tips and we'll also address a question we get a lot relating to whether the officer has to show you the radar gun.

First, let me address the distinction between radar and lidar guns.

Radar and Lidar also known as Laser are different types of speed measurements guns with different accuracy rates, and it's important that you take note of which the officer used, because he won't always make it clear on the ticket. In later webisodes we'll go more in depth into the distinctions between radar and lidar.

You have every right to ask to see the radar or lidar device but is the officer obligated to show you?

Not necessarily.

If it would compromise your safety or his safety to allow you to walk back to his patrol car while cars are whizzing by at high speeds, then your request will almost certainly be denied.

If the officer tells you that you can't see the device, don't argue, just make a note of it later on, especially if the officer doesn't state a reason as to why he didn't show you. For all you know the speed he stated he clocked you at really wasn't displayed on the device at all, and you can ask him to explain himself later if you decide to fight it.

If he does show you the device, remember you don't want to let the officer know you plan to fight the ticket. Just observe the device briefly and try to take a mental note of the make and model, so you can do your own research later on the accuracy of the model and under what conditions it is most accurate.

So remember, there is a difference between radar and lidar, and although you have a right to ask to see the device used to clock your speed, the officer is not obligated to show you.

Webisode #7 – Trial by Written Declaration Discussion
http://www.youtube.com/watch?v=ugNGC9CwHOc&feature=player_embedded

This week we are continuing our discussion detailing how to fight a ticket and get it dismissed by using a Trial by Written Declaration. In this fourth part of our discussion series, we will discuss how to complete a Trial by Written Declaration.

The first step of this process is to obtain the actual Trial by Written Declaration Documents. You can obtain these documents by going to www.TicketBust.com or any superior court web site.

A Trial by Written Declaration is a 2-page document. The first page is basic information about the court house, bail amount of your ticket and the due date of the ticket and looks like this. As you can see most of the information required can be found either on your actual ticket or the courtesy notice the court sends you.

If you are including any additional evidence with your California Trial by Written Declaration, you need to check the appropriate box at the bottom of this page.

Please note item "B-D" on the Trial by Written Declaration. One major requirement of a Trial by Written Declaration is that you post your bail with the court when filing a Trial by Written Declaration. This is a court requirement. As you will not be actually going to court to contest your traffic ticket, the court requires you to post your bail in order for the court to consider your Trial by Written Declaration

When the court receives your documents, the will cash your bail check and put it in their client trust account. If your Traffic Ticket is dismissed, the court will refund your bail to you in the form of a court check. If you traffic ticket is not dismissed they will convert your bail to the fine for the ticket and close your case.

In the next webisode of Ticket Talk we will talk about the second page of your Trial by Written Declaration and all subsequent pages that need to be submitted to the court.

Webisode #8 – How Radar and Lidar Can Vary
http://www.youtube.com/watch?v=mriqntzHDQY&feature=player_embedded

In a previous webisode of Ticket Talk we discussed whether an officer can refuse to show you a radar or lidar gun (the answer to which was yes) and we talked briefly about the differences between the two.

This webisode we will discuss in more detail how radar and lidar can vary.

Radar has multiple beams that can pick up all moving objects in range, where it is supposed to pick up the speed of the fastest moving target. Outside interference can affect the radar and it is generally less accurate from further away.

In order for the officer to clock you he will need a clear line of sight. There are certain conditions which are ideal for radar.

For example, a flat and straight road is ideal because of "terrain" error. This error can occur when you are coming downhill and there are cars behind you. The officer aims the radar at your car, but the radar is actually picking up on the car behind you.

For the officer to have a clear line of sight to your car there needs to be clear weather conditions and a fairly light amount of traffic. So if for example, it is dark and there is a lot of traffic, you stand a better chance at arguing the officer didn't have a clear line of sight.

Now you may wonder what the difference is between lidar and laser. There is no difference but generally if you receive a ticket from the CHP the ticket will usually say lidar and if you receive a ticket from say, a local police department it will usually say laser.

Lidar differs from radar because it uses a narrow light beam rather than multiple radar waves. The officer can clock you in a shorter amount of time with lidar, however it doesn't matter how accurate the laser is if the officer doesn't have a clear line of sight to a reflective surface on your car.

An easy target for the officer is your front license plate, so for example, if you are driving a car that is low to the ground and you are behind a tall truck then you have a good chance to argue the officer didn't have a clear line of sight especially if he had to aim across several lanes of traffic to get to you.

Webisode #9 – The Statement of Fact
http://www.youtube.com/watch?v=O7ZLT3HKpC4&feature=player_embedded

This week we are once again continuing our discussion detailing how to fight a ticket and get it dismissed by using a Trial by Written Declaration. This is the fifth part of our discussion series and today we will be talking about the second page of the California Trial by Written Declaration, the Statement of Fact.

Let's remind you how to obtain the actual Trial by Written Declaration Documents. You can obtain these documents by going to www.TicketBust.com or any superior court web site.

The second page of the California Trial by Written Declaration is the Statement of Fact. At the top of the page you must put your full legal name and your case or citation number. After that you will indicate your mailing address. This is the address that you would like the court to send any communications to, including your decision notice. This address does NOT have to be the same as the address on your driver's license; however it should be an address that mail is checked on a regular basis.

Next comes the Statement of Facts. This is where you will present your case to the court. Keep in mind that there is only a small space here so you will need to attach additional pages as necessary to explain your case properly. You should make sure that you present your case in a clear and concise manner. Take the time to make your points, but do not run on excessively as the court will lose interest.

If you need to attach additional pages, please make sure that you put your name and case or citation number at the top of each page and the page number at the bottom of each page.

Remember that you may attach any additional documentation as needed like, insurance certificates, driver's license, photos, certified letters or statements, diagrams, map and receipts if necessary.

Finally, please ensure that you do sign, print your name and date on this document. As we mentioned in previous webisodes you will send your Trial by Written Declaration to the courthouse indicated on your ticket or courtesy notice and it is always wise to send these documents to the court via Certified Mail.

Webisode #10 – Red Light Camera Tickets
http://www.youtube.com/watch?v=4kvAxluy8WM&feature=player_embedded

In previous webisodes of Ticket Talk we've talked a lot about speeding tickets so this webisode will be more geared to red light tickets. Specifically red light camera tickets because a lot of us are unfortunate enough to get them.

If you think there is no hope for getting a red light camera ticket dismissed and think the video and photograph they have says it all, you're wrong. Red light camera tickets are absolutely worth fighting!

Here's something to consider. If you're the registered owner of the vehicle pictured on the ticket and the ticket you received was mailed to you 16 days or more past the date of the violation, then you already stand a good chance at getting it dismissed on a technicality.

Take a look at the red light camera ticket you've received and look for the area titled "Certificate of Mailing". Listed here will be the date the ticket was mailed to you.

You'll want to compare this date to the date when the alleged violation occurred which is usually listed in the upper left corner. Should the date the ticket was mailed to you fall past 15 days after the date of the alleged violation, you're in luck. The California Vehicle Code, section 40518 (a) requires a written notice to appear based on an alleged violation of California Vehicle Code section 21453 to be delivered to the registered owner within 15-days of the violation.

This California Law gives police only a limited amount of time to deliver a genuine notice to appear to the registered owner. Logically this make sense because most people have no recollection of even going through a red light, so they should be given ample notice if they did, so they can remember where they were, what they were doing, or if someone else was driving their car at the time.

In future webisodes of Ticket Talk we'll continue to provide you with helpful tips and other relevant information related to traffic tickets issued in California. Remember that TicketBust.com can help you contest that speeding ticket, red-light camera ticket or other traffic infraction in the state of California.

Webisode #11 – Let's Talk About Cell Phone Tickets
http://www.youtube.com/watch?
v=sRr7MvK_mFQ&feature=player_embedded#at=16

Let's talk about cell phone Tickets. Everyone hates cell phone tickets but at the same time talking on a cell phone while driving seems like it has become a convenience that we can't seem to live without. Nobody will disagree that talking on a cell phone while driving is dangerous but so is eating while driving, changing the radio stations, looking for directions, putting on your makeup and even disciplining your kids in the back seat while driving.

Most people believe that cell phone tickets only cost you about $30-$40 and don't go on your driving record. This is not true. First of all, all cell phone tickets are reported to the DMV and WILL appear on your driving record. However, your first citation for using a cell phone ticket will NOT result in a violation point on your driving record.

Here's something new you should be aware of. The California Legislature has been trying to pass a bill that would make the first violation go on your driving record and also increase the fine for a cell phone ticket. If passed, this new bill would become law in July of 2011. Efforts to pass this bill into law, however, are still proving unsuccessful.

Currently the fine for driving while using a wireless phone is approximately $148 for the first offense and $256 for each subsequent offense in most counties in California. These are not inexpensive tickets. To be safe, we always advise using a Bluetooth while talking on a cell phone.

Next week we will answer some other questions about using a wireless phone while driving like:

- Can you look up directions on your phone while driving?
- Can you look up phone numbers and addresses while driving?
- Can you use your phones speaker phone while driving?
- Can you ever text while driving?

Webisode #12 – Commercial Drivers and Traffic Tickets
http://www.youtube.com/watch?v=7i-2FZ8na58&feature=player_embedded

If you're a commercial driver and received a traffic ticket in California, you will soon discover that you cannot just pay the ticket and attend traffic school like someone who has a regular driver's license. Even though commercial drivers are not eligible for a dismissal of their ticket through traffic school, there are other options for keeping the point off your driving record.

As a commercial driver, you drive for a living and most likely your livelihood depends on you having a good driving record, but going to court to try and keep the ticket from going on your record has it disadvantages. When you're trying to fight the ticket on your own you may not be sure of what to say or how to present your case to a judge, but more importantly you have to take valuable time off work that you should be out driving on the road, just to travel to the court and potentially wait for hours to state your case to a judge.

The best option for a commercial driver is to fight your traffic ticket using a Trial by Written Declaration. A Trial by Written Declaration allows you to contest your traffic in writing and it can be dismissed without you ever having to go into court.

Even if you feel you have no defense to fight your ticket and think there is no hope for keeping a point, or more, off your driving record, consider using a Trial by Written Declaration. Even if you have a log book ticket or an over weight ticket and you were clearly in the wrong, you may be surprised that your ticket could even be reduced to a no point violation if not completely dismissed after using a Trial by Written Declaration.

Webisode #13 – How to Handle Yourself During a Standard Traffic Stop
http://www.youtube.com/watch?v=PlhtCSVcsGc&feature=player_embedded

Back by popular demand, we'll be talking about more ways to best handle yourself during a routine traffic stop.

Let's talk about if you get pulled over at night. Naturally the officer will be more apprehensive since its dark and he won't be able to easily see into your vehicle. You can make the officer more comfortable by having your interior light turned on and both hands on your steering wheel when the officer walks up to your window. The more comfortable the officer is, the more smoothly the traffic stop goes, the more likely your chances of getting a reduced penalty or a warning. Of course, if *you're* at all apprehensive of the officer because he is in an unmarked vehicle or not uniformed, remember you can ask for identification.

You should remain in your car with the doors locked unless the officer tells you to get out. While in the car it's also a good idea to leave your seatbelt on. I cannot tell you how many people I've talked to who tell me they got a seatbelt ticket on top of the initial ticket that the officer pulled them over for in the first place. They take their seatbelt off before the officer walks up to the car in order to reach into the glove box and the officer walks up to see the driver's seatbelt is off and assumes it has been off the whole time. Don't let this happen to you. Take it from me its best to leave your seatbelt on and even better, ask the officer if you can remove it to retrieve whatever it is you need to retrieve that way he knows it was on.

We know viewers want to hear more on this topic and next week, we'll answer some other questions about getting pulled over, like how to respond to certain questions the officer may ask you.

Today we are continuing our conversation about cell phone tickets. Many people drive while talking on their wireless phone without a headset, speaker or Bluetooth device. Even worse, many people also text while driving.

The laws related to driving while talking or texting on wireless phone have changed over the last several years and if our lawmakers have anything else to say about it they will keep getting tighter and more restrictive, while also increasing the fines associated with these types of violations.

Today let's answer some questions about using a wireless phone while driving.

1. **Can you use your phones speaker phone while driving?**
   Yes you can use your phone's speaker phone, as long as you are NOT holding the phone.

2. **Can you ever text while driving?**
   As of January 1, 2009, the law prohibits all motorists from reading, composing or sending a text-based communication while operating a motor vehicle to manually communicate with any person. This includes text messages, instant messages or electronic mail.

3. **Can you look up phone numbers while driving?**
   Actually a person will NOT be deemed to be writing, reading, or sending a text-based communication if the person reads, selects, or enters a telephone number or name in an electronic wireless device for the purpose of making or receiving a telephone call.

4. **Can you look up directions on your phone while driving?**

   Let's think about this one as this is very interesting. We previously said that the law says that you cannot use your wireless device to manually communicate with another person. So if you are looking up directions, you are not communicating with another person so is this legal? Well the law isn't clear on this. As this might not be illegal, I would argue that it isn't safe and would advise against doing it.

Keep in mind that if you are under the age of 18, you can NOT use your cell phone for any purpose.

Today we are continuing our conversation about Cell Phone Tickets. This is the third part in our series on Cell Phone Tickets.

Previously we answered various questions related to the laws concerning driving while talking or texting on your cell phone. We've discussed how you can use your phone's speaker phone as long as you're not holding the phone and how you can look up phone number while driving as this is NOT considered reading or sending a text based communication.

Last week we also discussed that the law states that you cannot use your wireless device to manually communicate with another person. So we asked the question, can you lookup directions since you are not communicating with another person? According to Section 23123, you CAN send or receive wireless information that doesn't involve another person. This should mean that looking up directions or any other activity other than calling or sending information to another person should be legal.

Regardless of the actual law, it does appear that officers have been pulling drivers over even if they see the cell phone in their hand, regardless if they are actually using the phone or not. Technically, it is not illegal to hold the cell phone in your hand. It is only illegal to read something that was sent for communication by another person. Therefore it should be legal to read map directions or browse the internet.

When an officer sees a cell phone in your hand, he can't tell if you are texting or emailing another person or just looking up a phone number, an address, or directions. And since an officer can't actually tell what you are doing, he will usually pull you over and write you up for a cell phone violation regardless of whether or not you were doing anything illegal according to the law. It now becomes your responsibility to prove that you are innocent and will have to prove that you were not using your cell phone to communicate in any way with another person.

Webisode #16 – How to Best Respond to Questions During a Stop
http://www.youtube.com/watch?feature=player_embedded&v=Gumwk1d9CBw

Today, let's talk about how to best respond to certain questions the officer may ask you during a routine traffic stop.

First and foremost remember that most people cannot talk themselves out of a ticket. And, if you're not going to talk yourself out of a ticket at least don't talk yourself into a deeper hole then you're already in.

Try not to offer up any information unless the officer asks, and don't forget your right to remain silent. Should the officer ask you a question about the manner you were driving in and you feel compelled to answer, it's always good idea to keep your answers brief and as non-incriminating as possible.

For example, if the officer says "Do you know why I pulled you over". You could say, "No, I was driving safely". Or "Why didn't you stop for that stop sign?". You could reply "I did not proceed until safe". Or "How fast were you going? "A safe and reasonable speed". And don't think the officer will give you a break because you say you were only going 70 mph or even 66 mph when the speed limit is 65 mph, that's still speeding and you can bet the officer will write down what you've just said, if not on the front of the ticket, on the back of it so he can remember it later. A lot of people would also respond they were traveling "with the flow of traffic" and next week we'll discuss why this only counts in certain situations.

So, you can see, how you answer the officer's questions during a routine traffic stop is important, should you later decide to fight the ticket you don't want to give the officer extra ammunition to use against you.

Webisode #17 – Cell Phone Ticket Conclusion Part IV
http://www.youtube.com/watch?feature=player_embedded&v=pQ6sSuw7d18

Today we will conclude our 4-part series about cell phone tickets.

We've already found out that it IS legal to use your wireless device to manually communicate on the internet, look up direction and phone numbers as long as you're not communicating with another person. We also have discovered that you CAN use the phones speaker phone to communicate with another person as long as you are not holding the phone.

Today let's wrap up our conversation on wireless phones by asking these final questions:

1. **Can I use my cell phone during an emergency**
   Yes you can but you can only make emergency calls to law enforcement agencies, medical providers, the fire department, or other emergency agencies. Calling your kids, wife/husband or another person just to change or make plans is not an emergency.

2. **Can an officer pull you over for ONLY a cell phone violation**
   Yes, the police have primary enforcement authority for this violation and can pull you over for just this infraction. They do not have to see you doing anything other than using your cell phone to communicate with another person.

Let's also remember that it is NOT illegal to hold your wireless device in your hand while driving. However, when an officer sees that wireless device in your hand, he can't tell if you are texting or emailing another person or just looking up a phone number, an address or directions, or just holding it in your hand. And since an officer can't actually tell what you are doing, you're inviting him to pull you over.

My advice would be not to hold that wireless device in your hand and especially don't let an officer see it in your hand while driving.

Webisode #18 – Continued Tips for When You Get Pulled Over
http://www.youtube.com/watch?v=HuqrwPMdsz0&feature=player_embedded

Today, we'll continue our series on tips for when you get pulled over by an officer. Let's talk about more tips for when you get pulled over for speeding.

You should stay calm and signal when pulling over and pull far enough over so that the officer can stand by your car without getting hit.

During the course of the stop, try to figure out how the officer clocked you and note where he was when you first saw him. He may mention it while he's talking to you. For example, the officer may say that he clocked you and how, or he may say that he followed you, or that he was radioed in by another officer that clocked you. It may also say on the ticket he hands to you; on most tickets there is a box that says radar that the officer will check off or he can write in "laser", a pacing method or even an airplane, was used to clock your speed. If the officer just followed you to get your speed that way, you should try to take note of how long the officer followed you or if he just came out of nowhere and caught up to you very quickly.

My last bit of advice for today is that you should avoid admitting guilt to speeding or driving at any particular speed, either directly or indirectly. And one way you can indirectly state you were speeding is by telling the officer you were traveling with the flow of traffic, when say you were on the freeway, and the flow of traffic was well above the maximum posted speed limit.

Webisode #19 – Discussion on Red Light Photo Tickets
http://www.youtube.com/watch?v=qR5fBvIKbKk&feature=player_embedded

Red light cameras are all over the place these days. And I know most of us are thinking when we go through an intersection while the light is yellow and there is a camera, "is my picture going to be taken and am I going to get one of those Red Light Photo Tickets in the mail?"

Well, there is one group of people that never have to worry about receiving a Red Light Photo Ticket; this includes government and state workers.

Most people don't realize that California law allows "confidential license plates" are issued to police officers and all other state or governmental workers who request them. This allows them to keep their DMV information private.

The purpose of this law is to prevent disgruntled persons or criminals from harassing, threatening or stalking judges, police officers and other state and governmental workers. Over the years, this law has been expanded to include spouses and children and also allows them to retain their confidentiality for three years if they switch to a civilian job. The law also allows peace officers to remain in the confidential plate program indefinitely so certain private information like their home address and other public information is not released.

Since their home address is not released, there is no way for a Red Light Camera Agency to issue a Red Light Photo Ticket to any Governmental or State worker. And therefore they never have to worry about running a red light intersection that is enforced by a camera.

Next week we will take a more in-depth look at how this law works in relationship to Red Light Cameras and how this is affecting revenue for the state of California.

Webisode #20 – More Tips for When You Get Pulled Over by an Officer
http://www.youtube.com/watch?feature=player_embedded&v=-O8vxlABbvl

Today, we'll continue our series on tips for when you get pulled over by an officer. Let's talk about passengers in your car: If you get pulled over and have one or more passengers in your car, have them keep their seat belts on during the traffic stop, at least until the officer can clearly see into the car, otherwise its risky because the officer may walk up to the window of the car and assume the seat belts were off while you were driving.

You should also have your passengers remain silent, you don't want them to get into it with the officer and you don't want them to say anything that might incriminate you.

Lastly, your passenger can provide something very valuable to you should you decide to fight the ticket. They can provide a witness statement. This is especially helpful in situations where it's really your word against the officer's because you have another set of eyes to back up your position. Make sure that any witness statement you plan to provide to the court is notarized, otherwise for all the court knows, you wrote the statement yourself. It's worth paying a couple bucks to a Notary Public in order to make the witness statement credible.

Webisode #21 – Government and State Workers Part II
http://www.youtube.com/watch?v=Lkb9kt9XNP8&feature=player_embedded

Last week we spoke about how government and state workers never have to worry about Red Light Camera Tickets since the law

82

allows them to keep their DMV information private. Government and State workers: Part II This is the 2nd part in this series.

There is no question that camera enforcement of traffic violations generates millions in revenue for the State. There are currently over a million automobiles registered in the government and state workers' program. So theoretically this so-called loop hole could prevent the state from collecting on millions of dollars from those registered workers who are able to get around paying red light camera fines, tolls, or parking tickets.

Well, now law makers are taking notice of this potential funding source as efforts have been made to close this gap. Assemblyman Jeff Miller had sponsored a bill which would require confidential plate holders to supply a current employment address so that tickets could be mailed to that location. Initially this bill the was rejected, but Assemblyman Miller intends to reintroduce this bill in the future.

So what's the big picture? The confidential plate program allowing government and state workers to keep their DMV information private is bound to continue causing the State to lose out on revenue but overall it does not pose a major problem since the number of those violators that have confidential plates is really an insignificant amount when compared to the millions of motorists who are caught on camera committing a traffic violation each year.

Webisode #22 – Do You Have Control Over County Seat
http://www.youtube.com/watch?v=FR_WGPIZbLQ&feature=player_embedded

Today, we'll continue our series on tips for when you get pulled over by an officer. Let's talk about whether you have any say in choosing which court you have to appear in. We'll talk about what the term "County Seat" means and where some of the County Seats are located, why you should request it, who can request it, when you should request it, and what you can do if your request is denied.

You do have some say in choosing the courthouse you appear in, but this is limited to making a request to have your courthouse be where the "County Seat" is. Before making a request like this you should have some knowledge as to where County Seats are located. If there is a specific area that you frequent for work or school definitely look up the County Seats for those areas in case you're ever pulled over there.

What you should know is that every county has a County Seat and it is generally the largest city in the County. Occasionally the County Seat has the only court in the county so it won't do you any good to request it, or like in Los Angeles County, the entire city of Los Angeles is the County Seat so any of the branches within the City of Los Angeles are located at the County Seat. A simple online search of "California County Seats" should provide for you a complete list that you could print out and keep in your glove box for future reference. It's good to have a list to reference because if you get pulled over and you're already within the city where the County Seat is located or you are very near to it, it obviously won't do you much good to request it.

Webisode #23 – Number of Tickets Issued in California
http://www.youtube.com/watch?v=PDK5iO_yzxl&feature=player_embedded

Currently California issues approximately 16 million traffic violations every year. But even with so many tickets issued every year California ranks as only the 14th most likely state to ticket drivers.

The most common ticket issued in California is obviously a speeding ticket and we rank #4 among states most likely to issue a speeding ticket. The top 5 states that issue the most speeding tickets according to the National Motorist Association are:

1. Ohio
2. Pennsylvania
3. New York
4. California
5. Texas

California's largest county, Los Angeles, issues about 1.8 million traffic tickets every year.

One out of every six drivers will receive a traffic ticket each year.

About 5-6 million of the 16 million tickets issued every year in California carry only 1 point.

I hope you found these facts about traffic tickets issued in California interesting.

Webisode #24 – Requesting a County Seat
http://www.youtube.com/watch?v=vtsQGczJBLI&feature=player_embedded

Today, we'll continue our series on tips for when you get pulled over by an officer. Last week we talked about how you can choose to have the court at which you have to appear be in the County Seat instead of the courthouse the officer would normally write on the ticket. This week we'll take about the benefits of requesting the County Seat.

At the bottom of the traffic ticket there is a space for the officer to list the place to appear and this generally will be the court house located closest to where the officer pulled you over; usually within several miles of the traffic stop.

In general, the officer pulls you over in an area where he is based at so the court house written on the ticket will then be most convenient for him. In the event you have to go in to court to fight your ticket you want it to be at a place least convenient for the officer.

If the officer has to drive further to get to the court house, if he has to go to a court house he is not used to appearing in and go in front of judges he is unfamiliar with, then this could increase the chances of him not showing up in court. In the majority of cases where the officer doesn't show up, the case is dismissed.

So while it can be beneficial for you to request the County Seat remember to print out a list of the County Seats in California that way you don't waste your time if you were pulled over in a city that is the County Seat or if you were stopped in an area very near to the County Seat, because in those cases it won't make a difference.

Webisode #25 – Who Can Request the County Seat
http://www.youtube.com/watch?v=69ONUNB7kXY&feature=player_embedded

Today, we'll continue our series on tips for when you get pulled over by an officer. Last week we talked about how you can choose to have the place which you have to appear in be the County Seat instead of the courthouse the officer would normally write on the ticket. This week we'll talk about who can request the County Seat.

While it can be beneficial for you to request the County Seat it is important to know that not just anyone can request it.

If your home address is closer to the County Seat then the local court where you would otherwise have been told to appear, you can request the officer to write the place to appear on the ticket as the County Seat.

If your home address isn't close to the County seat you're not out of luck . You can still request that location if your business or work address is closer to the County Seat.

Webisode #26 – Car Pool Violations
http://www.youtube.com/watch?v=t2_E-isnKbg&feature=player_embedded

Here's a topic that several viewers have emailed us about, carpool tickets.

Traffic in California is terrible, and being stuck on a freeway while the cars in the carpool lane are zooming by is even worse. All of us at one point or another have thought to ourselves: "would it hurt if I crossed over into that carpool lane just this one time" even though you're driving alone.

We'll don't do it. Driving in a carpool lane with fewer than the required passengers is a very expensive ticket. The fine for this ticket can be up to $1,000. This violation is known as "Driving in the Carpool Lane Solo", code section 21655.5(b). However, this violation is a ZERO point violation, similar to your first cell phone ticket. The violation will show up on your driving record; however no points will be recorded.

There is one other type of Carpool violation, driving over the double yellow lines either in or out of the carpool lane. This violation also carries a hefty fine but unlike driving solo in the carpool lane, this violation WILL carry one point on your driving record as it is a more severe violation.

Our suggestion to you is never cross over a double yellow line, wait for the proper opening and make your legal lane change at that time. The few extra minutes it will take you to reach that point far outweighs the point on your driving record and hefty fine.

Webisode #27 – When to Ask for the County Seat
http://www.youtube.com/watch?v=Yh9g6nqCQ8k&feature=player_embedded

Today, we'll continue our series on tips for when you get pulled over by an officer. We've been talking about how you can choose to have the place which you have to appear in be the County Seat instead of the courthouse the officer would normally write on the ticket and last week we talked about who can request the County Seat. This week we'll talk about when this request should be made.

When the officer starts writing the ticket that is the time to make the request for the County Seat. You can tell the officer it is more convenient for you to have the place to appear as the County Seat. The officer may ask you why, and as we talked about last week if you live or work closer to the county Seat you have a right to request it. The officer may ask you for the business address to verify you actually do in fact work closer to the County Seat, or he may ask you for the residential address if it is different from the address on your driver's license.

If you sign the ticket without requesting the County Seat, you have promised to appear at whichever courthouse the officer wrote on the ticket. So, if you don't remember to make the request at the time the officer starts writing the ticket, then bring it up before you sign the ticket.

Webisode #28 – Parking and Stopping Infractions
http://www.youtube.com/watch?v=fCxrlv2_OAA&feature=player_embedded

Parking and stopping violations are usually not considered traffic infractions. However, there are a few parking and stopping violations that are considered traffic infractions.

The first violation is stopping at or on a bus zone. This is violation 22500(i). Yes, if you stop or park your car in an area where it is clearly labeled a bus zone you will be ticketed with an infractionable offense.

The next type of violation that is also considered an infraction is stopping or parking at a wheel chair access curb. This is violation 22500(l). There is also another violation related to wheel chair access, violation 22522, which is parking or stopping near a sidewalk ramp for wheel chair access. Both of these violations are considered traffic infractions.

All three of the above violations carry a hefty fine. This fine can be in excess of $1,000. This is not an inexpensive violation. However, even though the fine is large, none of the above violations will carry a point on your driving record.

Regardless of the fine and lack of a point on your driving record, this is basically just a safety issue. Drivers that are caught violating these laws usually just have a lack of respect for the law and common courtesy towards other drivers.

Webisode #29 – Nevada vs. California Tickets
http://www.youtube.com/watch?v=l1xmTHmx3el&feature=player_embedded

Here at TicketBust.com we have contested over 30,000 Tickets in California and many of those tickets are from drivers that do not live in California.

Since California is right next door to Nevada we see many tickets from residents of Nevada that happen to be driving back and forth between California and Nevada.

Many viewers have emailed us about the differences between California and Nevada traffic laws. So today let's take a look at one of the main differences in how you have to contest a traffic ticket in California as opposed to Nevada.

Nevada is a great state but they operate unlike many other states when it comes to their traffic violations. The bottom line is that in Nevada, just about any ticket can be changed to a Parking Ticket. Basically all you need to do is file some documents, pay your traffic ticket fine, and the court will change your traffic ticket to a parking ticket.

Since parking tickets carry no points, this ticket will not affect your driving record. Sounds like legalized bribery to me. All they want is your money. There are many companies in Nevada that will be happy to charge you a small fee to handle this for you and it is well worth that small fee.

In California, you cannot just pay the fine and have the court change your traffic ticket to a parking ticket. In California, you actually have to contest your traffic ticket either by going to court or filing a Trial by Written Declaration. We suggest that in California the best way to contest your traffic ticket is by using a Trial by Written Declaration.

This is usually sort of a shock to Nevada drivers that think that they can just pay the fine and make it go away by changing the ticket to a parking ticket.

Webisode #30 – Requesting the County Seat
http://www.youtube.com/watch?v=aA92YDkwnB8&feature=player_embedded

Today, we'll continue our series on tips for when you get pulled over by an officer. We've been talking about how you can choose to have the place which you have to appear in be the County Seat instead of the courthouse the officer would normally write on the ticket. Last time we covered this topic, we talked about when this request should be made. This week we'll talk about what you can do if your request for the County Seat is ignored.

If the officer ignores your request for the County Seat what you can do is write "County Seat Requested" beside your signature on the ticket. That way when you bring the issue up in court and request for the court to move your traffic ticket case to the County Seat, you have proof that you did in fact ask the officer at the time you were supposed to.

To recap what we've been talking about in this series:

1. You do have a right to make the request for the County Seat if you live or work closer to the County Seat,

2. Making such a request could inconvenience the officer enough that he doesn't show up on your court date,

3. The request needs to be made before the officer writes the ticket or right when he starts,

4. If your request is ignored you can make a note next to your signature,

5. It's a good idea to search online for county seat locations and keep that with you in your car, that way you don't waste your time making a request for the county seat when you were already in the county seat or it is very near to where you are pulled over.

Webisode #31 – Length of Yellow Light, Red Light Camera Tickets
http://www.youtube.com/watch?v=QVsEgt6stGk&feature=player_embedded

We've been talking a lot about traffic tickets that are handed to you by an officer so we're going to change it up this week and talk about Red Light Camera Tickets that are received in the mail. There some simple things you can do to better your chances at getting a red light camera ticket dismissed.

If you get a red light camera ticket one of the things you should do right away is go back to the location of the intersection listed on the ticket and time the yellow light. Many times cities make the length of a yellow light too short which can result in more people running red lights than can stop in time. Of course this is nothing more than a simple ploy to increase revenue to the city. So you want to make sure this didn't happen to you. Go back to the intersection with a stop watch and from the time the signal turns from green to yellow, begin timing until it changes from yellow to red. You'll want to do this a few times for accuracy.

Next you'll want to drive around and check for the posted speed limit on the approach to the light, the length of the yellow light depends on the approach speed (except in cases where you are making a right or left turn), and there are rules that say decreasing the length of a yellow light below the required minimum is not allowed. For example:

- If the posted speed limit on the street you were driving on is 25 mph (or less) the yellow shouldn't be less than 3.0 seconds and this includes both right and left hand turns as well.

- If the posted speed limit is 35 mph the yellow shouldn't be less than 3.6 seconds.

- If the posted speed limit is 45 mph the yellow shouldn't be less than 4.3 seconds.

Webisode #32 – Bail Is Required With a Trial by Written Declaration
http://www.youtube.com/watch?v=oMo4ylqY54w&feature=player_embedded

Here at TicketBust.com we complete and file Trial by Written Declarations on behalf of our clients to help them contest and dismiss their California Traffic Tickets.

One of the main requirements of filing a California Trial by Written Declaration is that you MUST post your bail, which is the fine for the ticket, with the court, in order to contest your traffic ticket.

Many of our clients have wondered: "why should I pay the court the fine for the ticket if I'm contesting my ticket?" The reason is simple. Since with a Trial by Written Declaration you will not be going to court, if you lose your case the court doesn't want to have to chase you down to collect the fine for the ticket. As such, they require you to post the fine with the Trial by Written Declaration and if the ticket is dismissed, the court will refund you the bail in full.

So logically our clients have also questioned the fact that will the court actually refund my bail. Then they think why would they dismiss the ticket if they already have the fine and then refund it. Fortunately, the California courts are very fair about this. They will refund your bail in FULL, 100% of the time if your traffic ticket is completely dismissed. That's the law.

So go ahead and contest your traffic ticket. You have nothing to lose by filing a Trial by Written Declaration.

Webisode #33 – How many Officers Need To Sign the Ticket
http://www.youtube.com/watch?v=EFOalbJ7p5c&feature=player_embedded

Today we are going to discuss a topic suggested by one of our viewers who asked, "When you get a speeding ticket, does the officer who got you on radar have to be the same one who gives you the ticket?"

If you look at a California Traffic Ticket you will notice that there are two spaces on a ticket for an officer's name. One space is for the citing or issuing officer, the other space is for an additional officer, if different from the officer who actually wrote up the ticket. So there can be two different officers involved when issuing a traffic ticket.

It's common practice to have two officers, especially for speeding tickets where a laser or radar device is used because the tracking device has to be used in a fixed location. This is how the process usually works:

The first officer takes the speed reading and the second officer is dispatched from the first officer to pursue the speeding car. The second officer then radios back confirmation to the first officer of the stopped vehicle. The second officer then makes the stop and issues the ticket. Both the first and second officers would also testify in a case like this if it went to court.

Webisode #34 – Better Your Chances of Getting Out of Red Light Camera Tickets
http://www.youtube.com/watch?v=d9NMUTqp-iA&feature=player_embedded

This week we're going to continue to talk about those red light cameras tickets that are sent in the mail. There are some simple things you can do to better your chances at getting out of a red light camera ticket. Last time we talked about why you should go back to the intersection and time the yellow light, this week we'll talk about what else you should check for at the intersection.

What a lot of people may not know is that it is required that cities post signs to warn drivers that certain intersections are monitored by red light cameras. Since this is a requirement, if you can find that this requirement has not been followed by the city in which you received the ticket, then this can definitely help your chances at getting your ticket dismissed.

When you go back to the intersection to time the light, at the same time you can check to see if there are any camera enforcement signs. If you don't see any at all or you see some but they are covered by trees, covered by graffiti, or bent over in such a way they cannot be seen then it's a good idea to take a picture with your camera so that you have proof there are no signs posted or proof that any signs there are not visible. Simple steps like this can really help your chances at getting out of a ticket like this.

Webisode #35 – One City Shuts Down Red Light Cameras
http://www.youtube.com/watch?v=mvGvKgwK2Ys

Red light Cameras are a very popular source of revenue for the state of California; however there are many communities and action groups trying to fight the legalities of red light cameras and get them shut down. In fact one city is set to shut down all their red light cameras effective June 1, 2011. That city is San Bernardino. Keep in mind that this is ONLY the city of San Bernardino not the County of San Bernardino. If you are driving in other cities within San Bernardino County you may still receive a red light camera ticket.

Many people may that if they received a red light photo ticket prior to June 1, 2011 it will just go away now that the City of San Bernardino is shutting down their cameras. This is not true. Even though there won't be any more red light camera ticket issued in the City of San Bernardino after June 1, 2011, any tickets where the date of the violation is prior to June 1 will still be valid even if you don't get the ticket or courtesy notice in the mail until after June 1, 2011.

Our advice to you is don't ignore that ticket if you receive one. However, don't just pay the ticket, contest the ticket.

We're going to keep on discussing those red light cameras tickets you receive in the mail because these can be tricky to deal with. Last time we talked about how you should check to see if there are warning signs posted at the intersection where you got the ticket. This time we're going to talk about what you should check for on the actual ticket.

A red light camera system at any given camera enforced intersection is supposed to be activated and enforcement is supposed to begin, when the traffic light turns red. These systems are not supposed to take a photograph during the time the traffic light is yellow or green. So, if a driver is facing a red light and enters the intersection the camera will activate and take a picture.

The "late time" or "red time" is the length of time the traffic signal was red before the vehicle entered the intersection. There are usually two red times. Once being how long the light was red before the vehicle entered the intersection, and the other being the length of time that elapsed between the time the first picture was taken (when the vehicle first entered the intersection) and the time the second picture was taken where the vehicle was actually traveling through the intersection. You definitely want to check the red time on your ticket because courts tend to be more lenient on drivers with very short late times (for example one tenth of a second or two tenths of a second).

Webisode #37 – What Is An FTA?
http://www.youtube.com/watch?v=JL8Eg5owg50

What is an FTA? An FTA is a Failure to Appear. This can happen if you have a court date or arraignment date scheduled and you do not show up in court. It's very important that you do not ignore any court notice or court date or you will be in jeopardy of receiving an FTA.

When you are pulled over for a traffic ticket you are required to sign the ticket. Signing the ticket does NOT mean that you are admitting guilt. By signing the traffic ticket you are only promising to appear in court by a certain date. This is stated on the back of the ticket.

What can happen when you receive an FTA? First of all whatever fine you had for that traffic ticket will surely be increased, and it can increase to over 3 times the amount of the original fine. Many times the court also refers the collection of the fine to a collection agency and you will start receiving many nasty letters and phone calls until this debt is satisfied.

If you failed to appear in court, the court will issue an FTA warrant. Now if you get pulled over for any reason, whether you are guilty or not, the officer can immediately arrest you and take you to jail.

 FTA's are extremely difficult to clear from your record. They are also considered misdemeanors and can appear on background checks. FTA's can also affect your ability to get a loan and your ability to afford insurance.

Our advice to you is never ignore any court date or court notice.

In future webisodes of Ticket Talk we'll continue to provide you with helpful tips and other relevant information related to traffic tickets issued in California. Remember that TicketBust.com can help you contest that speeding ticket, red-light camera ticket or other traffic infraction in the state of California. Go to our web site at www.TicketBust.com or call us at 800-850-8038

Until next time, this is Steve with TicketBust.com and this is Ticket Talk telling you to drive safely and if you do get a traffic ticket, TicketBust.com is on your side.

Webisode #38 – Is Window Tint Allowed?
http://www.youtube.com/watch?v=Qz2gGmP7Ed0

We've recently been contacted by a viewer who wants to know when window tint is and isn't allowed. Here at TicketBust.com, we have many, many people come to us with window tint tickets. Sure it looks cool but it can be costly if have it put on your car too dark or in the wrong place.

These tickets can be costly because you not only have to pay for the actual removal of the tint itself, but you also have to pay a correctable violation fee to the court, and have to waste your time driving to the police department to obtain a certificate of correction.

What most people don't know is that in California you are actually not allowed to have any tint on the front windows. You can tint the windows behind the driver and the back windows as long as you have side mirrors. In rare cases you are allowed to have front window tint but you will need a doctor's note saying you have a medical condition requiring you to be shielded from the sun and it has to be removed during periods of darkness, so that would really limit you to using pull down shades in the front windows.

Webisode #39 – LA City Turns Off Red Light Cameras
http://www.youtube.com/watch?v=MP6CJNTfoDQ&feature=related

Ok so here we go; another city has announced plans to stop using those red light cameras to enforce red light violators. But this time it's not just any old small city voting to stop using those cameras, this time it's the City of Los Angeles.

Currently the City of Los Angeles is scheduled to stop using those cameras by the end of July. By ending this program it would prevent the issuing of any future red light photo ticket. However, this does NOT mean that if you currently have a red light photo ticket that you can now just ignore it. All red light photo tickets issued prior the date the City of Los Angeles stops using these cameras are still valid tickets and they should not be ignored.

Even though the City of Los Angeles unanimously voted to end the program, two councilmen said that they would like to keep the program alive on a month-to-month basis for the next year.

This fight is not over yet. Stay tuned as anything can happen while the city looks for any way possible to raise money.

Webisode #40 – Correctable Violations
http://www.youtube.com/watch?v=SRhtj72-Dg4&feature=related

Today I want to go over correctable violations, because we are contacted by many potential clients that come to us about these.

Correctable violations do not result in points being added to your record. Speeding, Red Light, Stop Sign, Cell Phone, Unsafe Lane Change Tickets are generally NEVER correctable. Tickets for not having proof of insurance, or your front license plate mounted, etc., generally ARE.

Here's how to tell if your violation is correctable. Check your ticket in the same area you will find the violation code (generally right in the center of the ticket). There are boxes on the left side and if the 'Yes' box is checked then this violation is correctable.

If you were cited for not having proof of insurance but you DID have current insurance at the time then your violation should also be eligible for correction (even if the 'Yes' box isn't checked)upon showing your current insurance to the court.

For all correctable violations you will need to send to the court your Proof of Correction (proof violation was fixed or that you are no longer in violation) along with the fee the court charges. You will have to call the court to find out what the exact fee is, or check the courtesy notice sent to you by the court, but it is usually a nominal fee around $25.00.

If you are not sure what Proof of Correction is, here are some examples:

- Turn over the ticket the officer handed to you, there is a section marked "Certificate of Correction". Have this signed off by any law enforcement officer
- Car repair receipt
- Registration documents
- Insurance documents
- Copy of Driver's License

Webisode #41 – New Laws
http://www.youtube.com/watch?v=jMfSv81ooVo&feature=related

It's that time again when new traffic laws go into effect. Usually on the 1st of July and the 1st of January any new laws that have been past take effect. So here are a few of the new laws that have just gone into effect as of July 1, 2011.

1. Since 2008 using a mobile phone while driving has been prohibited. However, there was an exception for drivers operating commercial vehicles and equipment. They were allowed to use "push-to-talk" features on

their phone. Now effective July 1, 2011 this is also prohibited.

2. Previously cities and counties were allowed to pass ordinances covering violations that were identical to state law, such as obeying a posted traffic sign. By doing this local governments were able to boost their revenue because they would keep a larger amount of the traffic fine. Beginning July 1, 2011, local governments are now prohibited from creating identical violations to state law.

Webisode #42 – TBD What To Include
http://www.youtube.com/watch?v=B5XoYk2u4Us&feature=related

In the past we've talked to you about Trial by Written Declarations which is one of the best ways to get your ticket dismissed. Did you know that the average time a judge spends reviewing a Trial by Declaration is only about 5-10 minutes. This is why any statement you make on your Trial by Declaration should be done in an organized, easy to read, and easily understood manner.

Today I want to go over some of the things you should include in a Trial by Declaration:

- You should briefly describe what exactly you are being cited for

- Describe the surrounding conditions such as weather, traffic, and road conditions

- Describe where the officer was located and if there was anything in between you two that could have prevented the officer from seeing what exactly you were doing

- You can include any facts you feel are important, just try and keep from straying and stick to those facts that are relevant

- If there was an emergency situation causing you to do what you did, it is possible the court could see this as a valid excuse
- If there are any valid defenses that you can find that apply to you then include those as well

Next time we'll go over what NOT to include in a Trial by Written Declaration. Sometimes knowing what NOT to include is just as important as knowing WHAT to include.

Webisode #43 – New Laws Part II
http://www.youtube.com/watch?v=X2yUCadBbfY&feature=related

Last time we spoke about a few new traffic laws that went into effect as of July 2011. This week we will continue on with a few more of those new traffic laws.

1. Previously people were able to escape a second violation by taking traffic school. Effective July 1, motorists can only attend Traffic School once every 18 months and mask that traffic conviction. Previously when tickets were marked dismissed it was the same as a "not guilty" verdict so it appeared like you had no violations. Now frequent offenders are prevented from doing this and repeatedly attending Traffic School.

2. Drivers of Hybrid vehicles that had stickers that allowed them to be driven in carpool lanes, expired on 7/1/11. Electric and natural gas powered vehicles displaying white stickers may continue to drive in the HOV lanes until 1/1/2015.

3. The DMV has new services. You can now actually get a return call from the DMV. When you call, if the hold time is too long you can simply leave your phone

number and the DMV will call you back. Your call will stay in their queue and you will receive a return call. The DMV now also has self-service terminals for vehicle registrations and has added Droid & iPhone applications to facilitate their services.

Webisode #44 – What Not To Include In A Trial By Declaration
http://www.youtube.com/watch?feature=player_embedded&v=eRlMDytZETw#!

Last time we discussed that the average time a judge spends reviewing a Trial by Declaration is only about 5-10 minutes and we talked about some of the things to include in a Trial by Declaration.

Just as important as knowing WHAT to include in a Trial by Declaration statement is knowing what NOT to include, and today we'll go over this.

A Trial by Declaration statement:

- Should not contain lengthy discussion of irrelevant facts
- Should not bad mouth the officer
- Should not contain un-professional language
- Should not contain information about past violations or violations unrelated to the ticket you are currently fighting
- Should not be handwritten because you want it to be easily read
- Should avoid admitting guilt

Webisode #45 – Should I take traffic school or contest traffic ticket?
http://www.youtube.com/watch?v=QSa4G6IYJGg&feature=player_embedded

Hi this is Steve with TicketBust.com and this is Ticket Talk.

Should I take traffic school or should I contest my traffic ticket? Most people usually opt for the easiest choice, traffic school. But is this the best choice?

As many people know, in California you can only take traffic school once every 18 months. Since this is the case, wouldn't it make more sense to see if there was another option to get your traffic ticket dismissed other than traffic school? Yes! The best option is to contest your traffic ticket using a California Trial by Written Declaration. This is a way to contest your traffic ticket without going to court.

If your traffic ticket is dismissed, great no points go on your driving record and it's as if you never received the traffic ticket. This option also does not "mask" your traffic ticket with traffic school, insurance companies still see this ticket, but instead actually states that you are not guilty and insurance companies are not informed about this traffic ticket. You also preserve your right to traffic school in case you need to use it in the future. And if your traffic ticket is not dismissed then you can still request traffic school from the court if you are eligible. A Trial by Written Declaration should be your first option when receiving a traffic ticket.

So what's your best option if you receive 2 traffic tickets within a short period of time? We will discuss this next time on Ticket Talk.

Webisode #46 – Don't Just Pay A Traffic Ticket
http://www.youtube.com/watch?v=tCOtMLgOJ2U&feature=player_embedded

Hi this is Alexis with TicketBust.com and this is Ticket Talk.

Here at TicketBust.com we don't want you paying for a ticket when you don't have to! This is what today's topic is all about.

We have spoken with countless people who have gotten in the mail a notice from a police department or out of state camera company that is meant to fish for information, like your driver's license number, and to get you to tell on yourself (or someone else) for a red light violation. If you don't fill out the back of this notice and send it back to the agency requesting the information from you then they won't have enough to pin the violation on you and a get a real ticket issued to you through the court. Once you give up this information, the information can be used to get a real ticket filed with the courthouse.

A red flag should go up if you don't see a due date, a fine amount, and if you don't see a court house listed on the notice. If you are suspicious, check the notice for the city and county where the violation allegedly occurred (this will be on the front side of the notice listed along with information like the location and violation code). You can then go to the Superior Court website for that county and do an online search for the alleged ticket and fine information. You may be able to search by your driver's license, last name, or violation number. You could also try calling the court you think the ticket would have been issued in and inquire with a traffic clerk as to whether there is a ticket issued to you in their system, most likely there will not be.

If you're not sure of how to handle a red light photo ticket notice you received, before you do anything, it's a good idea to consult with a professional who is well seasoned with dealing with red light camera tickets.

Webisode #47 - Traffic School or Fight A Traffic Ticket - Part II
http://www.youtube.com/watch?v=pfBDDbeABpl&feature=player_embedded

Last time we spoke about your options to take traffic school or contest your traffic ticket? But what should you do if you received two traffic tickets?

Let's face it, one ticket sucks but if you receive two tickets you're really in a bind. As you can only go to traffic school once every 18 months to "mask" the traffic ticket, you obviously can go to traffic school on both tickets. Should you just choose traffic school for one of those tickets and either pay or contest the other ticket? Absolutely not!!!

If you just plead guilty on one of the tickets and accept traffic school on the other you just limited your options and you may have been able to get one of those ticket dismissed.

Here's what we suggest; complete and file a Trial by Written Declaration on BOTH traffic tickets. If they are both dismissed, great! If one of them is dismissed, also great as you can then elect to take traffic school on the other ticket. If neither of the tickets are dismissed, that's also ok because you are now right back where you started and you can then request a court date and negotiate with the judge to either dismiss or lower one of the tickets and take traffic school on the other ticket.

Webisode #48 - Traffic Ticket Points
http://www.youtube.com/watch?v=fYEwpY_kTys&feature=player_embedded

Today let's talk points.

The Department of Motor Vehicles will assess points to your driving record depending on the type of violation committed. What most people don't know is the number of points each violation carries and the length of time points stay on your record.

Violations such as driving by yourself in the carpool lane, driving without your seatbelt, driving without your driver's license in possession, and a first cell phone ticket are generally considered "zero" point violations as are violations committed while on foot or on a bicycle. While making an illegal pass, failing to yield to the right of way, exceeding the maximum speed of 55, 65, or 70 miles- per -hour are generally considered to be "one" point violations. The more serious offenses such as speeding over 100 miles- per -hour, driving on the wrong side of the road, and driving while on a suspended or revoked license are generally given two points.

The number of points on a driving record can affect not only insurance rates but also your driving privilege could be suspended or revoked if you accumulate 4 or more points in a 12 month span, 6 in 24 months, or 8 in 36 months. In addition, violations committed in a commercial vehicle carry 1 Â½ times the point count that would normally be assessed.

When weighing your options for handling a ticket it's also important to keep in mind that most one count violations will remain on a driving record for 3 years and the more serious 2 point violations generally do not fall off until 7 years after the date of the violation.

TicketBust.com Blogs and Articles

Everyone gets their information on the internet these days and business and personal blogs comprise a significant amount of the information. It seems that people just like to read about different topics from another person's perspective. And there's no shortage of people willing to write about various topics, even if they know nothing at all about that topic.

Fortunately, we like to write about various traffic ticket topics and unlike some people out there we know a thing or two about what we are writing about. You can find all the information we can share with you on our TicketBust.com blog at http://ticketbusters.wordpress.com/. Check back there once a week for new information, opinions and idle chatter.

Contesting over 30,000 tickets in California has made us an authoritative source for traffic ticket information on the internet. We have been featured on TV, radio, print and online magazines, and more.

To see what others have to say about us and catch up on everything we have to say too, keep reading.

Past TicketBust.com Blogs
11/3/10 - 2010 Marks the Year of the First Published Case on the Admissibility of Evidence in Red Light Camera Cases
Blog submitted by TicketBust.com, helping drivers contest and dismiss their traffic tickets.

Previously there was no case law on the subject of red light cameras and now finally there is. The case *People v. Khaled* (2010) 186 Cal.App.4th Supp. 1 was decided this year and is now precedent (pre decided cases on the same subject) to future red light camera tickets on issues relating to the admissibility of evidence and hearsay rules on red light camera ticket cases.

In *Khaled*, the court held that the trial court abused its discretion in admitting photographic evidence which contained hearsay evidence concerning the matters depicted in the photographs including the date, time, and other information--since the foundation for the introduction of the photographs and the underlying working of the automated red-light traffic enforcement camera system was outside the personal knowledge of the officer testifying in court--the evidence failed to establish each foundational fact and the photographs could not properly be admitted under any hearsay exception.

If the ticket mailed to you has a Certificate of Mailing stating it was mailed by an employee of the camera company and does not state that the camera company is a public employee or that they are otherwise employed by a public entity; if the person or persons who maintain the system do not testify; if no one with personal knowledge testifies about how often the system is maintained; if no one with personal knowledge testifies about how often the date and time are verified and corrected; if the custodian of records for the company that contracts with the city to maintain, monitor, store and disperse these photographs does not testify; if only the officer testifies on general information on how system worked based on his training and is unable to testify about the specific procedure for the programming and storage of the system information, then be sure to cite this case (case cite is *People v. Khaled* (2010) 186 Cal.App.4th Supp. 1) as reason why the citation should be dismissed.

The principals contained in the *Khaled* decision have created evidentiary hurdles for the Prosecution which could result in a significant number of red light camera tickets being dismissed.

11/3/10 - 2010 Court Decision Could Result in Significant Number of Red Light Camera Tickets Being Dismissed
Blog submitted by TicketBust.com, helping drivers contest and dismiss their traffic tickets.

People v. Park (2010) 187 Cal.App.4th Supp. 9, is a recently published case that can be cited and used as precedent (pre decided cases on the same subject) for all future red light camera tickets and luckily courts are to adhere to precedent under the legal principal of *stare decisis* (not unsettle things which are settled).

Park addresses the issue of warning requirements.

In *Park*, the defendant was ultimately found not guilty of violating VC§21453 because the photographs depicting the defendant's vehicle moving through a red light were gathered through an automated enforcement system whereby the issuing City of Santa Ana had not issued warning notices for "each new camera" installed in the city. This published court decision stands for the rule that the issuance of warning notices for the first camera installed in the City, and not for subsequent new cameras, does not satisfy the requirements set forth in VC§21455.5 (b).

If it comes up at your trial that the city that issued your ticket did not send warning notices for the camera which took your picture or for each new camera installed in the city, only the first one, then be sure to cite this case (case cite is *People v. Park* (2010) 187 Cal.App.4th Supp. 9) as reason why the case against you should be dropped.

11/9/10 - California Legislature Intends to Allow Street-Sweeper Automated Enforcement Systems: Assembly Bill 2567
Blog submitted by TicketBust.com, helping drivers contest and dismiss their traffic tickets.

The intent of this Bill introduced by Assembly Member Bradford this year, is to allow a parking citation for street sweeping violation to be issued, much like a red light camera ticket.

The ticket would be mailed to the registered owner of any vehicle parked during designated hours of operation for a street-sweeping parking lane, supposedly unless the vehicle is parked after the street is cleaned (even if this is during the restricted hours).

Just like the law for red light camera tickets, there would be a required public announcement of the automated parking enforcement system, a required 30-day grace period where only warning notices are mailed, only a designated and qualified employee could review the photos and the photo evidence would be confidential and available only to public agencies to enforce parking violations, and the ticket would have to be mailed to the registered owner within 15 days of the violation date. Just like with red light camera tickets, the registered owner would be given the opportunity to fill out and send back an affidavit of non-liability.

The legislature's reasoning is that street-sweepers collect excess pollutants from roads and streets like trash and chemicals which provides environmental and sanitation benefits which protects the environment and contributes to the general health of the people. According to an analysis by the District of Columbia Department of Public Works, a street-sweeper in a one mile range can remove approximately 10 pounds of oil and grease, pounds of nitrogen and phosphorus, and heavy metals. And the County of Los Angeles Department of Public Works submitted a technical report in 2004 pushing for stricter enforcement of "no parking" regulations and street-sweeping to help prevent harmful pollutants from entering storm water drains.

Street-sweepers play an important role in society but is the legislature going too far in allowing for the installation of camera enforcement systems on street-sweepers? It seems there's no end to what automated enforcement can be used for.

11/15/10 - Class Action Suit Seeks To Refund 3 Years' Worth of Red Light Camera Tickets Issued In Santa Ana, CA
Blog submitted by TicketBust.com, helping drivers contest and dismiss their traffic tickets.

The July 2010 Supreme Court decision (*People v. Park*) ruling in favor of the motorist ticketed for a red light camera ticket in Santa Ana, CA because the city lacked compliance with the requirement of Vehicle Code section 21455.5 (b) (that a municipality authorizing an automated enforcement system at an intersection comply with the prescribed warning requirements prior to issuing citations) appears to have opened the floodgates for litigation and paved the way for class actions law suits.

This is likely why the cities of Santa Ana, CA and West Hollywood, CA sent letters to the court in hopes of persuading the court to de-publish the decision, but it was to no avail as in October 2010, the Supreme Court denied the cities' requests for de-publication.

Now, motorist Robert Plumleigh was ticketed in Santa Ana at one of the sixteen camera enforced intersections where the city had failed to provide the required 30-day warning period, seeks to have all such illegally issued tickets refunded.

The suit seeks to refund tickets issued to motorists at the sixteen camera enforced intersections in Santa Ana, CA between May 2003 and November 25, 2009. The class action names the Santa Ana Police Chief, the Santa Ana City Attorney, and Red Flex (out of state camera company) as defendants, though Red Flex seeks to get out of the lawsuit, one reason being the warning period law allegedly does not apply to a private company.

Plumleigh's lawyer was given until December to file for class certification.

11/12/10 - What the Blank Data Fields on Your Automated Traffic Enforcement Notice to Appear Mean to You
Blog submitted by TicketBust.com, helping drivers contest and dismiss their traffic tickets.

A red light camera ticket is mailed to you on a form (form number TR-115) generally labeled Notice to Appear – Automated Traffic Enforcement. This form has data fields that are filled in with information like Name, Drivers' License No., Age, Birth date, Year of Vehicle., Make, Color, Code and Section, etc. Sometimes many of these fields are not filled in and you may wonder why.

Well, some of the fields are mandatory and some are optional or discretionary (like the color of the vehicle pictured). The Judicial Council of California, Notice to Appear and Related Forms available here: http://www.courtinfo.ca.gov/forms/documents/trinst.pdf, actually sets forth the mandatory fields which must appear and be filled in appropriately for the Notice to Appear to be considered genuine and valid.

Look to see if certain fields like your age and birth date are filled in or if the body style of your vehicle is filled in, if not, if these fields are left blank, then you might be able to get your ticket dropped on a technicality.

11/29/10 - Certain Group of Drivers Able to Avoid Getting Nabbed for a Red Light Photo Ticket
Blog submitted by TicketBust.com, helping drivers contest and dismiss their traffic tickets.

Approximately 30 years ago, the Confidential Records Program was started. Currently, CA law makes confidential license plates available to police officers and other state or government workers so they can keep info like their home address, and other data items that might appear on DMV related communications, private.

The law is supposed to keep certain information like, the home address, private to prevent, anyone from harassing, threatening, or stalking police officer's, judges etc. This law has been expanded over the years to include numerous other government or state worker positions, like park rangers, not just police officers or judges, and has even been extended to include spouses and children. Furthermore, employees can retain confidentiality for 3 years if they switch to a civilian job, and retired peace officers can remain in the confidential plate program indefinitely.

When someone in the privacy program is detected, the DMV can only release the person's employing agency to non–police agencies and or to private companies that process citations for cities and counties. DMV cannot release a home address and therefore a violator with a confidential plate who is caught on camera can go unscathed whether they intend to or not.

There is no question that camera enforcement of traffic violations generates revenue for the state, so if the DMV has a little more than one million vehicles registered to motorists which are connected to just a couple thousand state and local government agencies which are of those allowed to opt for confidential plates, theoretically this loop hole could prevent the state from collecting on millions of dollars from those state workers who are able to get around paying red light camera fines, tolls, or parking tickets. Assemblyman Jeff Miller has taken efforts in hopes to close this gap.

12/13/10 - Are Automated Traffic Enforcement Systems Speed Traps?
Technically Yes!
Blog submitted by TicketBust.com, helping drivers contest and dismiss their traffic tickets.

Red light camera systems are only supposed to record an incident that occurs during the red phase of the light, but ever wondered how the system is triggered?

A vehicle triggers the system by passing over a measured distance in the roadway (two sets of inductive loops are cut into the pavement). These sensors record the time it takes for the vehicle to cross the distance between the sensors and calculates the speed of the vehicle based upon the distance and the elapsed time for the vehicle to cross it. If the vehicle is over the set threshold then the system activates. Thus the calculated speed of the vehicle is used to trigger the camera (which records and stores information for use in later issuing a ticket for the prosecution of a red light violation).

California Vehicle Code defines a speed trap (in section 40802) as a section of a highway "measured as to distance and with boundaries marked, designated, or otherwise determined in order that the speed of a vehicle may be calculated by securing the time it takes the vehicle to travel the known distance". Speed traps are illegal in California.

So, red light camera system automated enforcement systems are technically illegal speed traps as defined in California law because of those sensors placed in the ground used to measure speed. Could this be a contributing factor to why class action lawsuits are finally being launched against major camera companies or why cities such as El Monte, Fresno, Moreno Valley, Union City and earlier this year, Costa Mesa, have shut down their camera systems?

12/20/10 - Distinction Between "Rolling Right" and Straight Through Violations
Blog submitted by TicketBust.com, helping drivers contest and dismiss their traffic tickets.

If you made a right hand turn at a red light and were nabbed by a camera, chances are that the ticket you received in the mail states you violated CVC§21453(a) even though they could have (some argue should have) cited you for CVC§21453(b). Here are both of these sections:

21453 Circular Red or Red Arrow

(a) A driver facing a steady circular red signal alone shall stop at a marked limit line, but if none, before entering the crosswalk on the near side of the intersection or, if none, then before entering the intersection, and shall remain stopped until an indication to proceed is shown, except as provided in subdivision (b).

(b) Except when a sign is in place prohibiting a turn, a driver, after stopping as required by subdivision (a), facing a steady circular red signal, may turn right, or turn left from a one-way street onto a one-way street. A driver making that turn shall yield the right-of-way to pedestrians lawfully within an adjacent crosswalk and to any vehicle that has approached or is approaching so closely as to constitute an immediate hazard to the driver, and shall continue to yield the right-of-way to that vehicle until the driver can proceed with reasonable safety.

Now, here's the distinction:

The first section (a) says nothing about right turns, and is basically used for those who go straight through a red light.

The second section (b) essentially says you can turn after stopping if there is no sign prohibiting a turn on red.

So if you made a "California rolling stop" why wouldn't you be cited for the second section (b) instead of (a) you might ask...

Check out this "Traffic Infraction Penalty Schedule" (from the January 2010 Edition Uniform Bail and Penalty Schedules, California Rules of Court, Rule 4,102):

Section: 21453 (a, c)
Offense: "Red" Signal- Vehicular Responsibilities

Total Bail/Fee (Keep in mind the so called "Total Bail" is before certain additional court or other fees that is added and there are 30 counties in CA authorized by law to exceed the total bail/fee):$380.00

Section: 21453 (b)
Offense: "Red" Signal- Vehicular Responsibilities With Right Turn

Total Bail/Fee (Keep in mind the so called "Total Bail" is before certain additional court or other fees that is added and there are 30 counties in CA authorized by law to exceed the total bail/fee):$146.00

So you can see the difference in bail amounts (fees) between the two is huge! For some cities, like Los Angeles most of the revenue is generated by right turns, in fact a Los Angeles Times article from December last year reported that according to the Los Angeles Police Department, an estimated 8 in 10 photo tickets were issued for right turns so it's no wonder police departments are issuing tickets under Vehicle code section 21453 (a) regardless of whether or not the motorist was turning right.

12/27/10 - What LA Courts are Doing if You Don't Pay Your Red Light Camera Ticket
Blog submitted by TicketBust.com, helping drivers contest and dismiss their traffic tickets.

Pursuant to a recent LA Times article about camera tickets, word has gotten around that LA courts don't report to the DMV if a person fails to respond to a Camera Ticket.

Some people are saying what's the point of fighting it then?

Well, if the registered owner fails to respond, the court will send a notice stating additional $300 will be imposed if not paid within 10 days. After that the registered owner's name is sent to collections. So although the DMV won't be notified to suspend the driver's license, a collections agency will be harassing them and could have a major negative impact on their credit score.

LA Superior Court may be one of the only counties, if not the only county, having this policy and it has this policy because in the court's opinion, since the registered owner may not necessarily be the driver it is not fair to suspend the registered owner's license without knowing they were the driver.

Keep in mind that the LA Times article is only specific to registered owners whose name appears on the ticket. So you will be taking a gamble if you are not the registered owner and your name was turned in by the registered owner and yet you still choose to ignore the ticket.

Also in choosing to ignore ticket and let collections come after them, all persons are taking a gamble that the court doesn't choose to change their policy at that time. It is a policy the court has elected to make, they were not mandated to do so, so really it could change at any time without notice.

1/3/11 - Check the Certificate of Mailing Date and Get Your Red Light Camera Ticket Dismissed
Blog submitted by TicketBust.com, helping drivers contest and dismiss their traffic tickets.

After a careful review of the red light camera ticket you've received, you will notice that there is an area titled "Certificate of Mailing" and listed here will be the date the ticket was mailed to you.

You will want to compare this date to the date when the alleged violation occurred (usually listed in the upper left corner). Should the date the ticket was mailed to you fall 15 days after the date of the alleged violation, then you'll be glad to hear the California Vehicle Code section 40518 (a) requires a written notice to appear based on an alleged violation of California Vehicle Code section 21453 must be delivered to the registered owner within 15-days of the violation.

This California Law gives police only a limited amount of time to deliver a genuine notice to appear to the registered owner. Logically this make sense because most people have no recollection of even going through a red light, so they should be given ample notice if they did so they can remember where they were, what they were doing, or if someone else was driving their car at the time.

So if you are the registered owner of the vehicle pictured on the ticket and the ticket you received was mailed to you 16 days or more past the date of the violation, then there is a good chance you can get this dismissed on a technicality.

1/10/11 - Registered Owner But Not the Driver and Not Sure What to Do?
Blog submitted by TicketBust.com, helping drivers contest and dismiss their traffic tickets.

If you're the registered owner of a vehicle and are being asked to identify the driver pictured on a red light photo ticket you are faced with several dilemmas.

Scenario One: Know the driver but don't want to turn them in. Filling out the affidavit may mean turning in a friend, family member, or even your own spouse. Say the driver was your spouse, but your spouse has more points on their license then you. It may make more sense to leave the ticket in your name. Deciding on whether or not to leave a ticket in your name and choosing not turn in the driver's name is up to you and legally you cannot be forced to identify the driver. See California Vehicle Code Section 21455.5(c) stating there is no requirement that the defendant bear any burden of proof in defending herself against a charge for violating California Vehicle Code Sec. 21453(a).

Scenario Two: Not sure who the driver is. On the other end of the spectrum you may very well not know who the driver is. Maybe you own a business and the car is used as a company car. Maybe you have a large family and multiple persons had access to the car. Perhaps the valet could have driven your car without you knowing it, or your car mechanic. In this situation you will not be able to complete an affidavit of non-liability truthfully even if you want to because there's no way to be exactly sure who was driving your car at that exact moment in time. Many courts will be understanding especially if the picture clearly does not look like you or there is a gender mismatch, but you stand an even better chance if you can back up your statement with proof. For example, find someone that is willing to testify as your witness that the car is driven by multiple drivers and it would be impossible to tell who was driving the car at that exact time.

Scenario Three: I can't tell if it was me or someone else driving. The picture may be too blurry for you to be able to identify the driver. In this situation it would be really difficult for you to complete an affidavit of non-liability because you would be taking a wild guess since you can't make out figure that is supposed to be a close up of the driver. If the picture is too blurry for you to make out the driver, there's a good chance the judge won't be able to either and you may be home free. If the picture of the driver is too blurry, the other side won't be able to prove that it was you driving. See California Penal Code Section 1096 stating that, in a criminal proceeding, the burden of proving the defendant's guilt beyond a reasonable doubt is upon the state.

1/17/11 - Short Red Time (Late Time) on Your Camera Ticket?
Blog submitted by TicketBust.com, helping drivers contest and dismiss their traffic tickets.

If you find yourself thinking you have no defense to a red light photo ticket, don't give up yet! You can still try to argue you could not have stopped safely within such a short time and short distance from the limit line and slamming on the brakes would have posed a greater danger to yourself and others than continuing through.

Look on your ticket for the late time (for example on a Red Flex ticket this will be displayed on the black bar across the top of the photos displayed vertically on the right hand side). If the red light camera ticket you received has a very short late time for example, one tenth of a second (0.1), wouldn't it have been very difficult to stop behind the limit line for the light when it changed? Even more so if it was raining. Perhaps slamming on the brakes would have resulted in you skidding into the middle of the intersection where you would have blocked traffic.

If your ticket does not show a late time then you can usually judge how long the light had been red by the position of other vehicles around you. If there were other vehicles turning left at the same time as you or going straight through and cross traffic hasn't moved past their limit line, then it's likely the light wasn't red for long at all. Of course if you were turning right, it's more likely than not that the light was already red and that you rolled through, so it's chancy if you don't have the red time.

The majority of tickets do show the red time and you stand a better chance if the red time is below five-tenths of a second (0.5) because although the law does not mandate them to do so, some local governments employ grace periods of up to 0.5 seconds before their red light cameras will begin taking photographs. Grace periods such as these are employed because it is understood that the shorter the red time the less likely the driver could have stopped in time. You stand an even better chance if that red time is three-tenths of a second (0.3) or below because as previously indicated by the Federal Highway Administration, a grace period of three-tenths of a second is commonly used and five-tenths of a second is the international standard.

1/24/11 - How to Begin Getting a Red Light Camera Ticket Dismissed
Blog submitted by TicketBust.com, helping drivers contest and dismiss their traffic tickets.

The first step to fighting any traffic infraction is to look up the vehicle code section you were cited with. The second step is to pick apart that vehicle code section in order to find out what the elements of the infraction are. If any of the elements necessary to be present in order to find someone guilty of the infraction are missing in your situation then you're well on your way to getting your ticket dismissed.

Now a red light camera ticket will have the violation code listed as California Vehicle Code (CVC) section 21453. You can go online to www.legalinfo.ca.gov to look it up. However there is more involved to fighting a red light camera ticket.

You not only need to look up that code section which you were actually cited for, but you also need to look up a few additional code sections, like what vehicle code section authorizes red light camera enforcement. Once you know what sections actually lay out the rules or requirements for the operation of red light cameras, you can write down those and then check to see if any of the rules were violated or requirements not followed in your case. Check out CVC§21453, CVC§ 21455.5, CVC§21455.6, CVC§ 21455.7, CVC§40518, if any rules listed in these code sections were violated, or requirements not followed, then you have ammunition for getting the ticket dismissed.

1/31/11 - Be Wary of Short Yellow Lights at Camera Enforced Intersections
Blog submitted by TicketBust.com, helping drivers contest and dismiss their traffic tickets.

If you get a red light photo ticket one of the things you should do right away is go back to the location of the intersection listed on the ticket and time the yellow light. Many times cities employ yellow lights that are too short in duration and which results in more people running red lights (and increased revenue to the city) because they couldn't stop in time-and you need to make sure this didn't happen to you.

Go back to the intersection with a stop watch and from the time it turns from green to yellow, begin timing until it changes from yellow to red. You'll want to do this a few times for accuracy. Jot down the yellow time and then make your comparisons.

The length of the yellow light cannot be just arbitrary. The California Manual on Uniform Traffic Control Devices ("MUTCD"), prescribes uniform standards for all official traffic control devices in California and the MUTCD section 4D-10 and Table 4D-102(CA), sets forth the minimum time for traffic signal yellow light change intervals. Section 4D-10 also provides that the time for a yellow light change interval may be increased through field review and appropriate judgment of the local agency. The MUTCD is very clear that increasing the yellow light interval above the minimum prescribed in the same section is an option and in no manner a requirement. Decreasing the yellow light interval below the minimum however, is not an option.

Check the Table (Table 4D-102) to see if the yellow light change interval at your intersection is non-compliant. Here are a couple examples of minimum yellow light times:

- If the posted speed limit is 25 mph (or less) the minimum yellow interval is 3.0 seconds (this includes both right and left hand turns).

- If the posted speed limit is 35 mph the minimum yellow interval is 3.6 seconds.

- If the posted speed limit is 45 mph the minimum yellow interval is 4.3 seconds.

2/7/11 - What You Should Know About Red Light Camera Tickets
Blog submitted by TicketBust.com, helping drivers contest and dismiss their traffic tickets.

Next time you get a red light ticket remember this. Red light camera tickets are very different from say a red light ticket handed to you by an officer. With a red light camera ticket, there is no "your word against the officer". With a red light ticket issued by an officer you have to try and convince the court that the officer did not have a clear line of sight to your car, to the limit line for the red light, or the red light itself, at the time you went through the light. Red light camera tickets on the other hand are best dismissed if attacked from a technical standpoint; after all it is a machine that ticketed you not an officer. And there are certain rules and requirements that are necessary to be present (or need to have been followed) in order for the red light camera ticket to be successfully held up in court against you.

For example there are rules regarding the length of yellow lights at camera enforced intersection, rules regarding how or when the actual notice of a red light camera violation is mailed out to the suspect violator, rules regarding what type of warning must be given about the presence or installation of a red light camera at an intersection, and rules regarding the types of fee arrangements cities having red light camera enforced intersections within their limits may have with private companies that manufacture and maintain the red light cameras. There is a lot of information out there available on the internet, so read about how these red light camera tickets work and learn what the rules are relating to them so that you can maximize your chances of getting out of a ticket like this.

2/14/11 - Where Camera Enforced Warning Signs Are Supposed To Be
Blog submitted by TicketBust.com, helping drivers contest and dismiss their traffic tickets.

Every wonder why there are warning signs for red light cameras at some intersections but not all? According to VC§ 21455.5(a) (1), "Warning signs must be posted at each camera-equipped intersection and visible to traffic approaching from all directions, or at all the main entrances to town including, at a minimum, freeways, bridges, and state highway routes." The purpose of the law is obviously to make sure that drivers are warned in all instances where there is red light camera enforcement, and the seemingly most obvious way to warn a driver is to post a warning sign say overhead on a traffic signal head, but the law doesn't require it.

The law does require that warning signs be posted, but the law gives cities the choice in where to post the signs and the law is vague as to how *close* to the intersection the signs have to be posted (provided the city decides to post the signs at the intersection). According to the Cal Trans design the signs must be at least 30 inches wide by 40 inches high and 6 feet off the ground but there is no requirement as to the distance a sign must be posted in relation to an intersection. Warning signs will not always be posted right at an intersection so drivers should be on the lookout for such signs when entering a city or exiting from a freeway off ramp. If you do get a red light photo ticket you should go back and search for warning signs and if you can't find anywhere they are supposed to be or the signs are there but they are not the right size or are blocked or damaged in such a way that they are not visible, then take photographs so you can dispute the ticket. If the signs weren't posted in accordance with the law (VC§ 21455.5(a) (1)) then as a result you weren't given the required notice and more importantly, a foundational requirement (warning signs) for the camera enforcement system is lacking.

2/21/11 - Will More Cities Follow Victorville's Lead?
Blog submitted by TicketBust.com, helping drivers contest and dismiss their traffic tickets.

At least three red light camera tickets issued in the City of Victorville have been thrown out by judges in San Bernardino Superior Court.

The City of Victorville has contracted with Redflex, an Arizona based, red light camera manufacturer, but as a result of court decisions proclaiming photographic evidence generated from the Redflex camera system as inadmissible evidence, the city is trying to get out of the contract. There are only 10 cameras left turned on in Victorville (out of the original 16) however if court decisions keep going the way they are going, Redflex may have to let Victorville out of its contract and Victorville could turn off the remaining 10 cameras making many citizens happy. In fact, according to the VVDailyPress.com, Victorville's contract with Redflex allows Victorville to get out of the contract if "any court having jurisdiction over city rules...that results from the Redflex System of photo enforcement are inadmissible in evidence".

A common factor in a lot of these Redflex camera ticket cases that have been dismissed is that no one from the Arizona based Redflex company attends the trials, the company instead sends a written statement as to how its systems work and an officer from the issuing city testifies on his training about how the system works and the photographic evidence presented. Many judges are refusing to consider this a proper way to authenticate the evidence (photos and videos). There is at least one published court case that discusses this same issue, *People v. Khaled.*

This leaves us to beg the question, will more and more judges follow the same lead these San Bernardino Superior court judges have taken? And will more and more cities take Victorville's lead in ending the use of these controversial camera enforcement systems?

2/28/11 - Benefits a Passenger can Provide if You Got a Camera Ticket
Blog submitted by TicketBust.com, helping drivers contest and dismiss their traffic tickets.

When a person gets a red light camera ticket, one thing often overlooked is the value a passenger can provide should you decide to fight a red light camera ticket. Anyone in the car with you at the time the picture was taken can provide a witness statement. This is especially helpful in situations where the weather conditions prevented you from stopping in time, there was a car tailgating preventing you from being able to stop short, or maybe there was a large truck ahead of you blocking your view of the light as it passed through the intersection.

In these situations, really all you have is your own word; however any passengers can back up your position. Make sure that any witness statement you plan to provide to the court is notarized, otherwise for all the court knows, you wrote the statement yourself. It's worth paying a small fee to a Notary Public in order to make the witness statement credible. Think about it, the court is on the fence as to whether or not to believe your story, having that witness statement to back up your story with, can give you that winning edge.

2/28/11 - How to Avoid Tattling on Yourself for a Red Light Camera Violation
Blog submitted by TicketBust.com, helping drivers contest and dismiss their traffic tickets.

If you receive a notice in the mail issued to you by a police department or even an out of state camera company what you shouldn't do is freely give them information requested of you. Often times these notices are sent out to fish for information, like your driver's license number, and to get you to tell on yourself (or someone else) for a red light violation.

A red flag should go up if you don't see a due date, a fine amount, and if you don't see a court house listed on the notice. If you're still unsure, check the notice for the city and county where the violation allegedly occurred (this will be on the front side of the notice listed along with information like the location and violation code). You can then go to the Superior Court website for that county and do an online search for your ticket and fine information. You may be able to search by your driver's license, last name, or violation number. You could also try calling the court you think the ticket would have been issued in and inquire with a traffic clerk as to whether there is a ticket issued to you in their system, most likely there will not be.

If not, then in that case, the ticket hasn't been filed or registered with the court yet so it's not an official ticket. Before you just roll over and comply with the first notice, you may want to wait and see if you ever do get a notice from the court, because you may not. If you don't fill out the back of the first notice and send it back to the agency requesting the information from you then they won't have enough to pin the ticket on you and a get a real ticket issued to you through the court.

If you're not sure of how to handle a red light photo ticket notice you received, before you do anything, it's a good idea to consult with a professional who is well seasoned with dealing with red light camera tickets. Remember, a ticket that hasn't been filed or registered with the court yet is not an official ticket and may never become one if you don't help them by tattling on yourself.

3/14/11 - If You're Caught on Camera for a Red Light Violation and You Were also on the Phone Can You Get a Ticket for Both?
Blog submitted by TicketBust.com, helping drivers contest and dismiss their traffic tickets.

If you've ever found yourself traveling through an intersection or turning at an intersection and being blinded by the flashing lights of the Automated Traffic Enforcement System at the same time as when you were on the phone, you may be worried that you will get a ticket for the cell phone violation as well as the red light violation. Well the good news is that so far, the vehicle section that authorizes a Notice to Appear to be mailed instead of handed to you by an officer, does not include the vehicle code section for cell phone use or texting while driving. So while you should always adhere to safe driving practices, you can rest assured that red light camera enforcement systems are not yet being used to also ticket drivers for cell phone violations. In any event, if an officer sees you on the phone, look out because with increased fines in California, the base fine (fine before other added court fees) for a cell phone violation used to be $20+ and it is now $80+.

*3/21/11 - Motorists Beware Camera Enforcement Systems Can Ticket
For More Than Just a Red Light*
Blog submitted by TicketBust.com, helping drivers contest and dismiss their traffic
tickets.

Whenever someone mentions they got one of those "photo tickets"
in the mail, everyone would assume it's a red light photo ticket.
However a red light violation is not the only thing that Camera
Enforcement Systems can be used for.

One should be especially wary at rail road crossings. The vehicle
code section governing stops at railroad crossings state in part:
"The driver of any vehicle or pedestrian approaching a railroad or
rail transit grade crossing shall stop not less than 15 feet from the
nearest rail and shall not proceed until he or she can do so
safely..."

Furthermore it states this relating to camera enforcement:
"Whenever a railroad or rail transit crossing is equipped with an
automated enforcement system, a notice of a violation of this
section is subject to the procedures provided in Section 40518."

What this means, in a nutshell, is that a ticket for failing to stop at
a rail road crossing can be mailed to you just like a ticket for failing
to stop at a red light, so drive careful you never know who, or
what, is watching.

*3/28/11 - Improper Right or Left Turn on Green Light Can Result in
Camera Ticket*
Blog submitted by TicketBust.com, helping drivers contest and dismiss their traffic
tickets.

Although there has been talk in California about allowing traffic
camera enforcement to be used for speeding, it is not yet allowed.
What is allowed is red light camera enforcement, of course, but
also the automated enforcement of certain turns made at an
intersection.

The California Vehicle Code section (40518) authorizing the use of a mailed notice to appear does include violations of 22101 recorded by an automated enforcement system and California Vehicle Code section 22101 does cover violations such as right or left hand turns that are prohibited by signs, disobeying traffic control devices, and other turning movements regulated by signs or marked traffic lanes.

That's right, you enter the intersection legally on a green light, but you might be making an illegal or improper turn. For that you could still get a surprise ticket mailed to you with a picture of you making that turn and for that you may get a hefty fine.

4/4/11 - Automated Traffic Enforcement of Seat belt Law
Blog submitted by TicketBust.com, helping drivers contest and dismiss their traffic tickets. Blog also submitted to photo enforced.com

Unlike Arizona for example, in California drivers cannot be ticketed for not wearing a seatbelt if their vehicle is photographed going through a red light. In Arizona if a driver is cited for the primary violation of running a red light or speeding, they can also be cited for a secondary violation like a seatbelt ticket or a ticket for expired registration. Californians are still only ticketed the old fashioned way, by an officer, for a seatbelt or expired registration ticket. It's a good thing too, because a red light camera ticket yields upwards of $400.00 plus a point or more on your driving record. To be ticketed for a seatbelt ticket in addition to the red light ticket would yield another $100 plus, as well as an additional point on your driving record. Drivers should always practice safe driving habits which would include wearing a seatbelt, but for now California drivers can rest easy as they will not be ticketed for a seatbelt ticket by a camera.

Blog submitted by TicketBust.com, helping drivers contest and dismiss their traffic tickets.

In California, anyone who receives a ticket for a traffic infraction can have the option to fight the ticket without going to court through a process called a Trial by Written Declaration. This is authorized by the California Vehicle Code, under section 40902 (a) (1). For those who receive a red light camera ticket, contesting the ticket through mail is a lot more appealing then showing up in person in court where there is an officer with a binder from the camera company who will testify on the workings of the red light camera.

When a person contacts a court to request a Trial by Declaration, the court will send you the necessary state approved forms for a Trial by Written Declaration (TR-205) and instructions. However if your red light camera ticket is filed with the Superior Court of Sacramento, this court tries to make it more difficult for you to contest your red light ticket with a Trial by Declaration.

The Sacramento Superior Court has a local form called a "Red Light Camera Statement of Identification" which states that "Without admitting guilt, I stipulate that I was the driver of the vehicle pictured in the automated enforcement photograph". The form itself does not state anywhere that it is mandatory it be filled out, and in fact the court website even only states, "...please complete the Red Light Camera Statement of Identification" (notice the use of the word please instead of must). However, if you don't complete this you could receive a notice of non-compliance or ineligibility after filing your Trial by Declaration paperwork and be dropped from the courts Trial by Declaration Calendar.

If you are not allowed to proceed with a Trial by Declaration then your only option is a court trial (outside of just paying the fine and accepting the points going on your record). But what if it is not convenient for you to appear in court because of your work schedule or the distance you live from the court? What if you were not the driver, but do not know who the driver is or you do know who the driver is but don't want to turn them in? Should you be prevented from using a Trial by Declaration simply because you cannot state under penalty of perjury that you were the driver?

With this unusual practice, the court is essentially saying that in order to avoid being dropped from the Trial by Declaration calendar, you must at least stipulate to one of the elements of the crime (identity – being the driver) which is an element that is supposed to be proven by the police department issuing the ticket, or your case will not be adjudicated (at least not by Trial by Declaration to which you have a right to contest your ticket by under 40902 (a) (1)). This unusual (dare we say unfair or unjust) practice has been in use for some time and those who are concerned about the matter might consider writing to or calling the head judge in Sacramento or the head office for all California courts in San Francisco.

4/25/11 - Fines for Red Light Camera Tickets Up From Last Year
Blog submitted by TicketBust.com, helping drivers contest and dismiss their traffic tickets.

According to the State of California Uniform Bail and Penalty Schedule, the base fine amount for a Red Light Ticket is $400.00. The base cost for the same type of ticket last year would have yielded $380.00. This $20.00 increase, added to the already extremely high fine for a red light camera ticket, is just another reason that many California motorists are opting to fight their red light camera ticket instead of just paying it.

The cost of your actual ticket will of course be more than the base fine after court fees are added. For example, a court security fee of $30.00 could be added and a conviction assessment of $35.00 could also be added in addition to the base bail.

Think the fines for red lights are already too high? Well, on top of the increase just from last year alone, there are certain counties in California (including Los Angeles, San Diego, Fresno County just to name a few) that are allowed by law to impose a fine which is greater than the base fine amounts listed in the Uniform Bail and Penalty Schedule.

5/2/11 – Bicyclists and Red Light Cameras
Blog submitted by TicketBust.com, helping drivers contest and dismiss their traffic tickets.

Most bicyclists are not aware that the motor vehicle code applies to them since they are not technically driving a motor vehicle. "Motor vehicle" would normally not be expected to include a device moved exclusively by human power.

Bicyclists however can be cited for a red light ticket under the California Vehicle Code due to the fact that, by statute, every person riding a bicycle upon a highway has all the rights and is subject to all the provisions applicable to the driver of a vehicle by this division.

Although a bicyclist could technically be ticketed by Red Light Camera, there is the simple fact that bicycles do not have a plate on them so the driver of the bicycle cannot be tracked.

State Assemblyman Michael Den Dekker in New York has introduced legislation that, poses the idea of requiring all bicycles to have a license plate, and placing cameras in the bike lanes, so that when a bicycle goes through a red light, they could be tracked down and issued a ticket essentially like registered owners of cars are tracked down and issued a ticket.

There doesn't appear to be any similar pending legislation in California like that in New York, however bicyclists in California do face hefty fines if ticketed by an officer (though no demerit points to their motor vehicle driving record).

5/2/11 – Do Cameras Shutting Down Have Any Effect on Your Current Red Light Photo Ticket?
Blog submitted by TicketBust.com, helping drivers contest and dismiss their traffic tickets.

It is rumored that the red light camera system for the City of San Bernardino (not the County of San Bernardino, just the City) is supposed to be shut down starting in June of this year. What you shouldn't do is assume that any current red light ticket you have from the City of San Bernardino will just automatically "go away" once the red light camera system ends.

Even though there won't be any more red light tickets issued in San Bernardino after June, be sure to take care of any outstanding tickets, because any tickets where the date of the violation is before June 1, should still be valid. For example the date of the violation may be May 31, even if you don't get the courtesy notice until July, it's still a valid ticket because the violation occurred before the city's red light program ended. Remember that the program is only supposed to turn off cameras in the City of San Bernardino, so still be wary of the camera enforced intersections through other areas of San Bernardino County where the cameras are still turned on.

5/12/11 – How to Read a West Hollywood, San Francisco Red Light Photo Camera Ticket
Blog submitted by TicketBust.com, helping drivers contest and dismiss their traffic tickets.

Not all red light camera tickets are the same as there are different red light camera companies. Some are easier to read then others. If you have ever received a Red Light Photo Ticket in cities like West

Hollywood and San Francisco you may have had difficulty trying to figure out what all those numbers mean at the top of your photograph.

Cities like West Hollywood or San Francisco use the technology of ACS camera systems and on these camera tickets there is a photo of the vehicle's position when the light first turns red and a picture of the vehicles position when it is going through the intersection. There is a square block at the top center of each photograph. There are numbers and symbols listed on these square data blocks that translate into things like the speed of your vehicle at the time you passed through the intersection, the date of the violation, and the timing of the traffic signals.

If you are looking at the square data block on the first photograph, it is important to know that the first set of numbers is the time of day, the set of numbers to the left of this is the Date/Month/Year. The next line of numbers reflects how long the light was yellow before the light turned red, and the last set of numbers to the left of this reflect how long the light was red before the vehicle entered the intersection.

As for the data box on the second photograph, it is important to know that the first row of numbers here is also the time and date. The second and third rows are a little different though. The second row tells you how much time has passed in between Photograph One of the vehicle and Photograph Two, how long the light has been red between Photograph One and Two. On the third and final row, there is the violation counter (if there was only one person that ran a red light ahead of you then the violation counter will read 002), and the last set of numbers reflects the speed of your vehicle. If you plan on fighting your ticket then it definitely helps to understand what all those numbers mean.

5/16/11 – What is meant by Red Time on a Camera Ticket?
Blog submitted by TicketBust.com, helping drivers contest and dismiss their traffic tickets.

A red light camera system at any given camera enforced intersection is supposed to be activated and enforcement is supposed to begin when the traffic light turns red. These systems are not supposed to take a photograph during the time the traffic light is yellow or green. So, if a driver is facing a red light and enters the intersection the camera will activate and take a picture.

The "late time" or "red time" is the length of time the traffic signal was red before the vehicle entered the intersection. There are usually two red times. Once being how long the light was red before the vehicle entered the intersection, and the other being the length of time that elapsed between the time the first picture was taken (when the vehicle first entered the intersection) and the time the second picture was taken where the vehicle was actually traveling through the intersection. It's a good idea to check the red time on your ticket because courts tend to more lenient on drivers with very short late times (example one tenth of a second or two tenths of a second).

5/26/11 – What to do When a Camera Ticket has an Unclear Photo of You
Blog submitted by TicketBust.com, helping drivers contest and dismiss their traffic tickets.

Those red light cameras tickets you receive in the mail can be tricky to deal with. Many find themselves stuck with a ticket that says they were the driver but doesn't actually have clear photo of the driver's face.

If you receive a ticket in the mail that says you were the driver but it doesn't have a clear picture of your face it can be frustrating because without a clear picture how can you even tell if it was you driving? There is a way you can send in a form saying that someone else was the driver, but with a blurry picture how can you tell who it is.

You could, of course, go into court and let a judge see for himself that there is no possible way you could be identified as the driver based on the picture on the ticket. You could also explain to a judge that you can't identify anyone else as the driver because of the poor picture quality. But going into court can be a hassle and scary for some, so it's much easier to handle situations like this without going into court, with a Trial by Written Declaration. Using a Trial by Written Declaration you can explain the situation and even include a recent photograph of yourself for the judge to use as a comparison to the picture of the driver on the ticket. In situations like this there is a good chance your ticket will be dismissed.

6/6/11 – Constitutionality of Red Light Cameras Being Scrutinized Once Again
Blog submitted by TicketBust.com, helping drivers contest and dismiss their traffic tickets.

Since the development of automated traffic enforcement questions have been raised and lawsuits have been launched to challenge the constitutionality and fairness of these systems.

Just last month, an attorney in Orlando, Florida spoke out in court arguing the red-light camera law is unconstitutional. For a long time running, many have felt the system robs individuals ticketed of the constitutional rights to due process and equal protection under the law. It is rumored that several other attorneys with clients that have received a red light camera ticket will also go to court this June to argue their cases. This could be the beginning of a statewide revolt against red light cameras that could certainly turn nationwide if word gets around to enough disgruntled motorists

6/13/11 - How Changes to Traffic School Laws Will Affect Those With Multiple Red Light Camera Tickets
Blog submitted by TicketBust.com, helping drivers contest and dismiss their traffic tickets.

There is a new law effective July 1, 2011 that will affect CA Traffic School laws. Say you get multiple red light camera tickets within an 18 month period, well there will no longer be the possibility of taking traffic school more than once. Whereas before repeat violators could still take a Traffic School course if the court allowed it, now the courts will no longer be able to exercise this type of discretion.

The law will no longer allow superior courts to "mask" a conviction as a dismissal after traffic school is taken IF there is already a "masked" conviction on a person's record within the previous 18 months. So you are still allowed one in 18 months, but there is no chance you can do Traffic School multiple times any more.

Basically the purpose of the law is to prevent the Courts from allowing repeat violators more than one Traffic School dismissal within 18 months, so drivers should be aware of this new law, always remember to drive safely, and take special caution at camera enforced intersections.

6/20/11 - Even if LA Shuts Down Red Light Don't Forget About the One You Already Have
Blog submitted by TicketBust.com, helping drivers contest and dismiss their traffic tickets.

As many of you may know, Los Angeles has announced plans to stop using cameras to enforce red light violators at numerous intersections throughout the city. While many are rejoicing that the cameras may be shut down by the end of June, don't forget about the red light ticket you currently have! The program ending would prevent future red light camera tickets from being issued but don't assume that any current red light camera ticket you have from the City of Los Angeles will just automatically vanish if the red light camera system ends. To avoid potential problems be sure to follow up on any outstanding tickets. You can always check the status of your ticket on the court website to see if it is still active or closed. Remember if the ticket is already filed and active with the court before the city's red light program ends (if in fact does end), then it may not automatically be dropped and if you don't follow up on the ticket it may go to collections or affect you negatively in other ways if the DMV is notified (LA courts exercise their own discretion and can choose to refer your information to a collections agency or the DMV or both, although it is rumored they usually stick with the first option).

6/27/11 - Why Every Camera Enforced Intersection Doesn't Have Warning Signs Posted
Blog submitted by TicketBust.com, helping drivers contest and dismiss their traffic tickets.

The California Vehicle Code only requires that warning signs be posted to notify drivers of camera enforced intersections and that these signs be posted either at all approaches to the intersection or at all main entrances into a city including (freeways, bridges, and state highway routes).

Many times you will see warning signs posted right next to the traffic signal light, however not always. Sometimes warning signs might even be posted at the previous, non-camera enforced intersection which can be misleading or cause confusion. So while a city may not be in violation of the Vehicle Code requirements if they don't have warning signs placed at the intersection (since they have a choice in the placement), if any signs you do find are blocked or damaged in a such a way you can't see them, then you may have something that can help you in getting your ticket dismissed because warning signs do have to be reasonably visible. Be sure to take pictures of the signs to show they are not visible and take them to court with you or include them with your Trial by Written Declaration if you choose to fight your ticket in writing using form TR-205 (available at your local courthouse).

7/4/11 - Knowing What To Include In A Trial By Declaration Statement Is Crucial For Successfully Fighting Your Traffic Ticket In The Written Form
Blog submitted by TicketBust.com, helping drivers contest and dismiss their traffic tickets.

A Trial by Written Declaration is one of the best ways to get your ticket dismissed. Did you know that the average time a judge spends reviewing a Trial by Declaration is only about 5 to 10 minutes. This is why any statement you make on your Trial by Declaration should be done in an organized, easy to read, and easily understood manner.

A few things you should include in a Trial by Declaration statement:

- You should briefly describe what exactly you are being cited for

- Describe the surrounding conditions such as weather, traffic, and road conditions

- Describe where the officer was located and if there was anything in between you two that could have prevented the officer from seeing what exactly you were doing

- You can include any facts you feel are important, just try and keep from straying and stick to those facts that are relevant

- If there was an emergency situation causing you to do what you did, it is possible the court could see this as a valid excuse

- If there are any valid defenses that you can find that apply to you then include those as well

Knowing what to include in a Trial by Declaration statement is crucial for successfully fighting your traffic ticket in the written form.

7/11/11 - Why Parking Tickets Cannot be Contested Using Trial by Written Declaration
Blog submitted by TicketBust.com, helping drivers contest and dismiss their traffic tickets.

A Trial by Written Declaration is one of the best ways to get your ticket dismissed however not all tickets can be contested using a Trial by Written Declaration.

To name a few, red light, speeding, cell phone tickets are all types of tickets you can contest using a Trial by Written Declaration. Only traffic infractions can be contested using a Trial by Written Declaration, and parking tickets generally cannot be due to the following:

Years ago, Assembly Bill 408 revised and recast procedures for processing and adjudicating parking law violations. The bill required courts to transfer the processing of parking ticket to the issuing agencies and consequently parking violations were no longer cited as a traffic infraction.

There are a very small number of parking violations that, by law, are still allowed to be cited as an infraction. A violation of disabled parking, parking in a bus loading zone, parking at a wheel chair access curb, and parking near a sidewalk access ramp for disabled persons are those parking violations that an officer can exercise his discretion and choose to cite as an infraction. If the officer did cite you for one of those parking violations and indicated he was citing it as an infraction then you would be able to contest it using a Trial by Written Declaration.

7/18/11 - Bicyclists Can be Cited For Red Light, Stop Signs Tickets and More
Blog submitted by TicketBust.com, helping drivers contest and dismiss their traffic tickets.

By law (California Vehicle Code section 21200), "Every person riding a bicycle upon a highway has all the rights and is subject to all the provisions applicable to the driver of a vehicle by this division, except those provisions which by their very nature can have no application." Essentially this means that cyclists are to act and be treated as drivers of cars. However many inexperienced or non professional bicyclists are not aware that the vehicle code applies to them while they are on a non-motor driven device, moved exclusively by human power. Unfortunately, this is no excuse, and while it may seem unfair, bicyclists (of any level of experience), are expected to know the rules of the road and abide by them.

It is true a driver of a bicyclist can be cited for a red light, a stop sign violation, for wearing ear plugs in both ears while riding, etc. What's more, is that many of the violations committed while on a bicycle will carry a point (or more) and can affect your driver's license and insurance rates. Luckily a ticket issued to a bicyclist can be fought or contested in the same way as a ticket received while driving a car.

7/25/11 - Knowing What Not to Include In A Trial By Declaration Statement Is Just as Important For Successfully Fighting Your Traffic Ticket In The Written Form
Blog submitted by TicketBust.com, helping drivers contest and dismiss their traffic tickets.

A Trial by Written Declaration is one of the best ways to get your ticket dismissed and since the average time a judge spends reviewing a Trial by Declaration is only about 5–10 minutes, knowing what to include in a Trial by Declaration statement is crucial for successfully fighting your traffic ticket in the written form. It is however just as important to know what not to include.

A Trial by Declaration statement:

- Should not contain lengthy discussion of irrelevant facts
- Should not bad mouth the officer
- Should not contain unprofessional language
- Should not contain information about past violations or violations unrelated to the ticket you are currently fighting
- Should not be handwritten because you want it to be easily read
- Should avoid admitting guilt

8/1/11 - What to do With Outstanding Red Light Tickets For City of LA
Blog submitted by TicketBust.com, helping drivers contest and dismiss their traffic tickets.

The City of Los Angeles ended its red light camera traffic enforcement program yesterday, Sunday July 31, 2011. With regard to whether outstanding Los Angeles City Red light Camera tickets need to be dealt with still, the short answer is yes. Although at least one Los Angeles City Councilman has hinted otherwise, Los Angeles Superior Court says different. According to a statement made by the court on its website, "The City of Los Angeles has decided to end its red light camera program on July 31, 2011. The City's action does not stop the processing of outstanding red light citations. It does not eliminate penalties associated with red light citations. It does not constitute grounds for a refund of any money paid on such a citation. Anyone issued a red light citation must resolve it within the specified time limits or face certain penalties as prescribed by law." The court has made clear that drivers can still be penalized for outstanding red light tickets issued in the City of Los Angeles. Driver's that don't want to just roll over and pay the exorbitant fine for these tickets have options for fighting these tickets by either a court trial or a Trial by Written Declaration and with a Trial by Written Declaration you won't have to waste your time going to court since no appearance is required for a Trial by Written Declaration. Information on how to request for or file a Trial by Written Declaration can be found on the TicketBust.com website at www.TicketBust.com.

8/15/11 - Speed cameras on Ramona Expressway?
Blog submitted by TicketBust.com, helping drivers contest and dismiss their traffic tickets.

While driving on the Ramona Expressway, Highway 371 in Anza, or Highway 60 (between Moreno Valley and Beaumont) you may have seen what looked to be photo radar enforcement and had that sinking feeling that you would be receiving a ticket in the mail.

In reality, a motorist driving a bit too quickly through those areas will see a "slow down" message flash and a white light pulse, which is what, may be confused by some as a camera taking a picture. In reality these are just radar speed feedback signs and no ticket will result.

In fact, the speed cameras (which would allow speeding tickets to be issued by mail much like red light cameras) have not yet been legalized in California and even the recent AB 1311 Bill which sought to legalize speed cameras in California did not make it out of the Assembly by the deadline.

8/23/11 - Lower Speed Limits?
Blog submitted by ticketbust.com, helping drivers contest and dismiss their traffic tickets.

In California we have a basic speed law, that no one can driver at a speed which is unsafe for the surrounding conditions. We also have default speed limits. 25 on residential streets. Can't go more than 55 mph on other roads even if no speed limit is posted. And no more than 65 mph on the freeways, unless there's a posted 70 mph sign.

What if a local government wants to set a speed limit lower than the default 55 mph? There has to be a survey done in which several factors are looked at to determine the correct speed for that road. Every several years, a city traffic engineer goes out to the street and uses a radar gun to measure the speed of say 100 cars. The speed of the 15 fastest cars is discarded and the speed of the fastest car remaining is the "85th percentile speed."

As the law is currently, if the 85th percentile speed of free flowing traffic on the road is 38 mph, the engineer must round up to 40 mph. A new Assembly Bill (AB 529) if passed would allow the city engineer to, instead of rounding up, to round down. Instead of having to round up to 40 mph from 38 mph the speed limit could be posted at 35 instead.

8/29/11 - Speed cameras on Ramona Expressway?
Blog submitted by www.ticketbust.com, helping drivers contest and dismiss their traffic tickets.

While driving on the Ramon Expressway, Highway 371 in Anza, or Highway 60 (between Moreno Valley and Beaumont) you may have seen what looked to be photo radar enforcement and had that sinking feeling that you would be receiving a ticket in the mail.

In reality, a motorist driving a bit too quickly through those areas will see a "slow down" message flash and a white light pulse, which is what, may be confused by some as a camera taking a picture. In reality these are just radar speed feedback signs and no ticket will result.

In fact, the speed cameras (which would allow speeding tickets to be issued by mail much like red light cameras) have not yet been legalized in California and even the recent AB 1311 Bill which sought to legalize speed cameras in California did not make it out of the Assembly by the deadline.

9/7/11 - Don't Wind Up Paying for A Ticket You Didn't have to in the First Place
Blog submitted by www.TicketBust.com, helping drivers contest and dismiss their traffic tickets.

You don't want to wind up paying for a ticket when you didn't have to in the first place do you? This is a topic we have blogged about in the past but it's important enough to revisit, because too many people receive notices from police departments or out of state camera company that are meant to fish for information, like your driver's license number, and to get you to tell on yourself (or someone else) for a red light violation.

Either on the notice itself or an attach page, will be blank lines with fields for you to fill in. If you don't fill out the back of this notice and send it back to the agency requesting the information from you then they won't have enough to pin the violation on you and a get a real ticket issued to you through the court. Once you give up this information, the information can be used to get a real ticket filed with the courthouse.

Be very suspicious if you don't the court house listed on the notice. Be wary if you don't see a due date. Be careful if you don't see a fine amount listed. You could even go so far as to go on the website for the court in the county the violation supposedly occurred in and do a search for the ticket. You could also try calling the court you think the ticket would have been issued in and inquire if there is any record of a ticket being issued to you, most likely there will not be!

Red light camera tickets can be tricky so it doesn't hurt to get professional help.

9/13/11 - Avoid High Fine Carpool Tickets
Blog submitted by www.ticketbust.com, helping drivers contest and dismiss their traffic tickets.

Driving in heavy Los Angeles traffic can be a real nightmare but worse than that is getting a carpool lane ticket. Hybrid drivers could once enjoy riding in the carpool lane even if they didn't have a passenger so long as they had a yellow carpool lane sticker however that luxury expired earlier this year in July. Currently Natural Gas Vehicle drivers, Compressed Natural Gas Vehicle drivers, and Pure Electric Vehicle drivers can drive solo in the carpool lane until 2015 (with a white carpool sticker). As for the rest of us driving without a passenger in the carpool lane can result in an exorbitant fine.

If you do get a carpool ticket there are ways to fight it, and although driving by yourself in the carpool lane will generally not result in a point going on your driving record (it is a zero point violation versus driving across double yellows into or out of the carpool lane will result in a point) the fines for a ticket like this can range from $400 on up. Keep your hard earned dollars in your own pocket by staying out of the carpool lane if you don't have a passenger or white carpool sticker, don't risk having to fork it over to the state.

9/16/11 - Commercial Drivers Who Drive Too Fast Face Serious Consequences
Blog submitted bywww.ticketbust.com, helping drivers contest and dismiss their traffic tickets.

Did you know that if you hold a commercial driver's license and drive a commercial vehicle at a speed of 15 miles per hour or more above the posted speed limit for trucks with trailers that you can be cited for a misdemeanor? It's true!

The officer can choose to cite you for the usual violation for speeding in a commercial truck, California Vehicle Code section 22406 (which is an infraction) or he can choose to instead cite you under section 22406.1 (a) of the California Vehicle Code which is a much more serious offense!

Don't risk it! If cited for the latter you could be facing serious consequences such as a suspended driving privilege, jail time, or outrageous fine.

Articles

Fees on Traffic Tickets Skyrocketing in California
BBB Clears the Air on Driver Advocacy Firms Claiming to get
Consumers out of Tickets

By Scott M. Aronson, BBB Editor
May 9, 2011 Santa Barbara, CA

Municipalities throughout California are levying record fines
against drivers for routine traffic infractions. In the past four years,
the most common traffic fines have more than doubled. What was
once a $249 red light violation is now $500-$600, and drivers
can expect to pony up an estimated $1,800 in increased insurance
premiums over a 3-year period for each point on their driving
record. Given the State's ongoing fiscal budget crisis, this trend of
increasing fines is expected to continue with the 18 million tickets
estimated to be issued in California this year, just 9% of which will
be contested by drivers; of those, about 25% will be contested
through a legal procedure that is quickly gaining popularity,
known as 'Trial By Declaration', or more formally, 'Trial By
Written Declaration'(TBWD). Only about 6 states currently offer
its citizens the TBWD option. CA is one.

Whereas in the past, a driver often just reluctantly paid a traffic
fine regardless of whether they were guilty of the infraction,
today's driver is forced to explore all of their options before writing
that exorbitant check.TicketBust.com,the nation's premier driver
advocacy group, is helping drivers to do just that.

Founded in 2004, TicketBust.com, a Better Business Bureau
Accredited Business with an A+ rating, assists drivers with
fighting speeding tickets and other traffic tickets by using proven
legal methods. One such method, Trial By Written Declaration,
allows for a driver to contest with the court a traffic ticket by mail.
According to Steve Miller, CEO of TicketBust.com, which also
offers multilingual versions of its service viacombatesuticket.com
and byebyefadan.com, "Millions of drivers are completely unaware

150

that they have a legal right to a trial by written declaration...if they just look at the reverse side of their ticket, they will see this as an option to contest their ticket."

In the BBB's own investigation, we found what may be contributing to consumers from fully understanding their right to a TBWD. In examining the back of a traffic ticket issued to a BBB employee, we noticed the TBWD option stated clearly and conspicuously. However, the courtesy notice that was mailed to the BBB employee, when examined closely, was shown to make no mention whatsoever of the TBWD option. The BBB believes that since a large contingent of drivers rely upon the courtesy notice that is mailed to them and not the ticket itself, this may be perpetuating the lack of public awareness on this issue.

Miller, a former CPA who ran a web-based applications firm in the dot.com boom era, was inspired in 2004 to launch TicketBust.com after learning that his brother successfully beat a ticket by utilizing his right to a trial by written declaration. In his research, he learned that there was nothing else out there in the marketplace that facilitated the contesting of a ticket. Miller then set out to develop a proprietary system whereby for a $100 service fee, and $149 document processing fee, TicketBust.com handles almost all of the details regarding ticket contesting. The streamlined process allows consumers to complete a 1-2 min. online form which prompts TicketBust to conduct a short 5-10 minute fact gathering telephone interview with the client. Then TicketBust writes a strategically-worded and customized written declaration that gets submitted to the court, along with the client's fine/bail check, which is refunded to the driver if the ticket is dismissed.

According to the company, the hallmark of TicketBust's service offering is its expertise, which is evidenced by not only their A+ BBB rating and high success rate, but also in their willingness to offer a money-back guarantee. TicketBust now boasts an impressive client list exceeding 30,000, though this number continues to grow quickly as an increasing number of drivers beat their tickets and then spread the word to their friends, colleagues and family."

In response to increasing consumer awareness and demand for this type of service, brand new firms with little or no experience are popping up on the scene. Therefore, the BBB urges consumers to be cautious and recommends that they know who they are dealing with before paying any fees. Consumers should check with the BBB to verify if the company they are considering is legitimate. If a company has both a high rating and is accredited by the BBB, then consumers can rest assured that they are dealing with a firm that will likely lead to a positive outcome.

One measure the BBB uses to assess the legitimacy of firms is length of time in business, as the longer a firm is in business, the likelier it is that they are credible. In fact, the BBB recently declined accreditation to a new firm in this industry that had no relevant prior experience or industry background for that matter. "What we have here are people with limited knowledge attempting to pass themselves off as experts by taking peoples' money without really knowing what they are doing. This is unacceptable because so much is riding on it for the driver."

This is certainly not to say that companies new to the ticket dispute arena are all incompetent. As we learned in our interview with Miller, many of these newer firms may know what to say in their clients' TBWD. But according to Miller, and more subtly, knowing what not to say in a TBWD declaration is even more important, and can only be learned over a substantial period of time. Further, the data in a TBWD must contain many critical facts that must also be organized in such a way that a judge wants to see it. TicketBust's approach has been modified and developed over time, and one of their strategies is to always stay abreast of the constantly-changing laws. "Our Goal at TicketBust is to help as many people as possible understand that they have rights. We will do everything in our power to maximize a consumer's chance at a successful outcome by guiding them through the TBWD process every step of the way."

Consumers, it should be pointed out, can also consider going it alone in disputing their tickets through TBWD without hiring a firm like TicketBust, but their chances at having the ticket dismissed are diminished greatly. The BBB cannot stress enough that the ticket disputation process is a very meticulous one that must be taken seriously and requires expertise. As Miller puts it, "You can fix a broken pipe in your home, or you can call in an expert—a plumber. The same principle holds true here. In this same way, we are the experts, as having literally, invented this industry".

Trial by Declaration: Several Facts

- California drivers have the legal right to dispute minor traffic violations/infractions through a TBWD
- Municipalities in California offer the TBWD as a way to alleviate what are now overbooked court dockets
- Diver must pay bail amount that goes into trust account to be refunded upon not-guilty court decision
- If a driver is found guilty, they still have the right to a court trial and traffic school
- Driver effectively is in no worse shape if they lose their TBWD, as they effectively get "2 chances at the legal system".

The Ticketbuster
Westlake Village firm fights for its clients

By Marlize van Romburgh
Staff Writer

TicketBust has crafted a company by helping to get California's accused speed demons off the hook.

The Westlake Village-based firm, founded in 2003, claims to have been the first of a handful of online companies that have sprung up offering money-back guarantees for getting clients out of speeding and red-light tickets.

The firm, which said it has processed more than 27,000 California traffic tickets since its inception, calls itself a "legal document filing" service. It's careful not to claim to be a law firm or legal service, which would require bar association oversight, but does say that it's competing against ticket-fighting attorneys for what appears to be an ever-growing market.

"I figured there are a lot of people out there who have no clue about how to contest a ticket," said Steve Miller, a former accountant who started TicketBust after he created an interactive advertising agency that went under in the dot-com crash.

"People, a lot of times, are confused about what to do when they get a traffic ticket," he said. "Look at your options. There's a lot of ways to legally fight a ticket."

Miller said he became a ticket-busting businessman after his brother came to him and explained how he'd managed to get out of a traffic ticket. "He got rid of his ticket without even going into court. It was all done in writing, through something called a 'trial by written declaration,'" Miller said.

He decided he could make an online application that processed large volumes of written declarations for people who couldn't or didn't want to deal with the hassle of paperwork themselves, but who also didn't want to pay expensive attorneys' fees, fight the ticket in a courtroom, or just pay up and let it go.

"The moment for us, when we realized we were on to something, was this: Over 16 million tickets are being given out in California every year. And nobody has even heard of a trial by declaration, which is something every driver has a right to do," Miller said.

A big chunk of the firm's revenue comes from the commercial sector — taxi, truck and limousine drivers who can't afford to get points on their licenses.

Traffic tickets aren't cheap. Fines can often top $400, and TicketBust says that according to its research, drivers see their insurance premiums increase an average of 27 percent for a single ticket and up to 40 percent for a second offense.

"People are fed up with the price of a ticket," Miller said. "They believe that the governments, state and local, are just gouging them."

TicketBust charges $100, refundable if the ticket is not dismissed, plus a $149 nonrefundable "document processing fee."

Miller estimated that his firm gets 60-80 percent of its customers' tickets dismissed, but he said not all clients report back with the results after their case is over.

The art of ticket busting The TicketBust model isn't entirely welcomed by the legal community. Jay Leiderman, a criminal defense attorney with Leiderman Devine LLP in Ventura and the information officer for the Ventura County Criminal Defense Bar, said that while online traffic ticket-fighting sites rarely bite into an attorney's business, he tells clients to be wary of such services.

"We attorneys tend to view these types of Internet-based corporations with a bit of distrust until they sort of prove otherwise," he said. "I would proceed with caution with a company that's making guarantees and has hidden fees."

At the same time, a service like TicketBust isn't competing with most criminal defense firms. "I don't see it as something that cuts into my business. I would only do a traffic ticket for a friend of mine for free. It's just not cost-effective for us to do a traffic ticket. Someone isn't going to pay $500 or $1,000 for us to spend three to four hours fighting a ticket," Leiderman said.

But there are attorneys who do make their living from fighting traffic tickets, he said. Like TicketBust, those lawyers have generally found a way to process large volumes of tickets in a relatively short amount of time.

"There's an art to fighting a traffic ticket," Leiderman said. "There's no question about that."

'Busto mi ticket' Drivers who use TicketBust's site start by clicking a big button that says, "Bust my ticket now!"–or, on the Spanish version of the site, *"Busto mi ticket ahora!"*

The customer submits some information about the citation and signs off to its accuracy. The eight-member TicketBust staff researches the case and files the necessary documents with the court. Meanwhile, the court looks through the written declaration filed by TicketBust and makes its decision. The officer who wrote the ticket has to dispute the points made in the declaration–failing to do so can get the ticket dismissed, Miller said.

If TicketBust customers lose with the written declaration, they can still go to court to fight the ticket in person.

After seven years in business, TicketBust is expanding its offerings and breaking into new demographic markets.

The firm recently launched a Spanish speaking division, www.CombateSuTicket.com. "I see that as a huge market," Miller said. "It seems like a lot of people like to speak in their native language whether they can speak English or not. We wanted to cater to that Latino market."

Since launching the Spanish service in fall 2010, TicketBust has hired two bilingual employees. The company will be also launching Chinese and Korean sites in coming months, Miller said.

California Morning TV Anchorman Steve Schill Brings Hope to Drivers by Praising TicketBust's Traffic Ticket Service

FOR IMMEDIATE RELEASE, Westlake Village, United States, 06/30/2010

TicketBust.com is a document processing and filing service that files documents on behalf of their customers, like Steve Schill, Morning TV Anchorman, to assist them in getting traffic tickets dismissed. They do this by filing a Trial by Declaration, a legal process to contest a traffic violation in California. TicketBust handles all the paperwork and submits these documents on their client's behalf so that they don't have to appear in court. In many cases, the tickets are dismissed and TicketBust clients do not receive points on their driving record, nor do they have an increase in their insurance premium. The interview below describes how TicketBust was able to help Steve Schill with his traffic ticket needs. This interview will appear on TicketBust's Blog and is scheduled for release through PRWeb.

QUESTION: Mr. Schill, why did you agree to interview with us today?

Schill: "I went 20 years without getting a ticket. Last year I was pulled over by a local police officer in my town after he used radar to estimate my speed. I was convinced the officer and his radar gun were wrong and needed some help fighting the ticket. I didn't know where to turn ...so ... I went to the internet and did some research. I was relieved to find TicketBust.com."

QUESTION: While at KMIR 6, TicketBust's President Steve Miller had a guest appearance on your morning show. Can you describe how that came about?

Note: Mr. Miller was a wonderful guest. Very informative and offered people an alternative to simply "laying down" and accepting the ticket (and the consequences.. fine, points, higher insurance rate). Currently Steve Schill now works with KPSP Local2, CBS TV.

Schill: "TicketBust worked for me and I wanted to share my good fortune with my viewers. I invited TicketBust's President, Steve Miller, to talk about what TicketBust does, and how they beat tickets for Californian drivers." Mr. Miller was a wonderful guest. Very informative and offered people an alternative to simply "laying down" and accepting the ticket (and the consequences.. fine, points, higher insurance rate)

QUESTION: Why did you feel so compelled to have Steve on your show?

"I needed someone to fight for me without the service costing me an arm and a leg. I thought many Californians were unaware of the services provided by TicketBust and wanted to help drivers reduce or eliminate ticket fines. As so many drivers do, I was going to avoid the hassle and just pay the citation. Then I realized that my excellent driving record would be blemished and frankly, I didn't want the points on my driving record as well as an inflated insurance premium. Also, I was in the right. It seems fairly clear that cities, towns, counties and states are seeking revenue and one of their primary sources is drivers that "they say" broke the law. Think of it as a public service.

Because you did such a wonderful job for me, I wanted to offer the same services to our viewing audience. You have a money back guarantee, and right away when I saw that, I said 'what have I got to lose!"

QUESTION: And you ended up with how many tickets?

Schill: "I ended up getting two more tickets within a one year period. Another for speeding and one for turning right on a red light (camera took a picture of me!!!) TicketBust beat them all."

QUESTION: After working with TicketBust on two more tickets, do you have anything else to add regarding your recent experience?

Schill: "Yes, I ended up with three tickets; one red light camera ticket and two speeding tickets. Since the Ticket Bust service is a no lose proposition, I hired them to help with all of my traffic tickets. Thank God for TicketBust!!!! I hadn't got a ticket in 20 years and then three years ago I got a speeding ticket. I contacted TicketBust and they got my ticket dismissed. Then a few months later a traffic camera claimed I turned illegally on a red light. I got the ticket in the mail and immediately called TicketBust. Dismissed!!!

"Recently another speeding ticket on I 5. The CHP was right behind me and wrote me up. I thought sure I was busted and couldn't beat this one, but I thought what the heck ... Contact TicketBust .... I just learned today ... The ticket was dismissed, but just the same I am more careful and a better driver in part due to the great team of experts at TicketBust. Drive carefully, but don't give up if you do get a ticket!"

If you too would like to share information about this unfamiliar and underused legal California service with your listeners or viewers, please contact Steven Miller at the number below.

Videos and Links

TicketBust.com dismissed 4 tickets for the NBC Newscaster – Click on the link to watch TicketBust.com interviewed live on NBC
http://www.youtube.com/watch?v=lykV4r3XbJw&feature=player_embedded

My Local Buzz TV (mylocalbuzztv.com) features TicketBust.com as the the company leading the way assisting driver's to contest their traffic tickets by using a California Trial by Written Declaration. They state it's the best way to contest a traffic ticket in California
http://www.youtube.com/watch?v=PtUXRm8_BC0&feature=player_embedded

Steve Miller, CEO, speaks on KFWB News Talk 980 AM on the Penny & Phil Show *Providing His Expertise on Contesting Traffic Tickets.*
http://ticketbust.com/radio/index.asp

Steve Miller, CEO, speaks on the Karel Show as an expert on traffic tickets for Energy 92.7 FM.
http://ticketbust.com/radio/index.asp

BBB Interviews TicketBust.com to Inform Public of Legal Rights Concerning Fighting Traffic Tickets - Click on the link to read full story
http://www.santabarbara.bbb.org/BusArticle.aspx?ID=2000163

"A Better Way To Fight A Traffic Ticket" Commercials
TicketBust.com has released a series of new commercials centered around their new marketing campaign "There's Gotta Be A Better Way To Get Out Of A Traffic Ticket." Click on the video links to watch all 6 TicketBust.com commercials:

TicketBust.com - "A Better Way To Fight A Traffic Ticket" - Dog Lover
http://www.youtube.com/watch?v=M4jCiAtPQxo

TicketBust.com - "A Better Way To Fight A Traffic Ticket" - Hottie TV
http://www.youtube.com/watch?v=8Rvb58HZQ2k

TicketBust.com - "A Better Way To Fight A Traffic Ticket" - Business Woman
http://www.youtube.com/watch?v=rtSlc5YM5mQ

TicketBust.com - "A Better Way To Fight A Traffic Ticket" - Plumber
http://www.youtube.com/watch?v=KZ-iqT3Q_wg

TicketBust.com - "A Better Way To Fight A Traffic Ticket" - Handyman
http://www.youtube.com/watch?v=5_7SWvNAvWY

TicketBust.com - "A Better Way To Fight A Traffic Ticket" - Business Man
http://www.youtube.com/watch?v=MgY-7uvNvXY

Introducing iTicketBust *– The first mobile APP to contest and dismiss your California Traffic Ticket – AND IT'S TOTALLY FREE*
http://www.ticketbust.com/app-page.html

Definitions to Commonly Used Traffic Ticket Terms

General traffic court terminology and traffic terms broken down into plain English.

Acquitted The court has declared that you are innocent.

Appearance Date This is the date listed on your ticket or courtesy notice. You must take some sort of action by this date whether it is submitting a Trial by Written Declaration, making an appearance in court or paying the cost of the ticket, it has to be done no later than this date.

Appeal If you are dissatisfied with the decision a judge made after a court trial you are sometimes able to file an appeal to try and have that judge's decision overturned. Appeals are often complex and complicated and most people have an attorney assist them with it, although you can contact the court for the necessary paperwork and filing deadlines.

Arraignment This is just a court appearance where you can tell the court how you intend to plead (i.e. guilty/not guilty). This isn't an actual trial where the officer is present. If you want a court trial or Trial by Written Declaration you can request one at this time and you'll be given a new date to appear for the trial.

Bail This is the cost of the ticket as determined by the court. If you plan on fighting the ticket, it's referred to as bail because you can potentially be refunded the money you paid the court if your ticket is dismissed.

Bailiff maintains overall courtroom order, security and custody of the jury. In Traffic Court, this is the officer who will take any documents needed from you and provide them to the Judge.

Calendar The cases set for hearing or trial in a specific department, on a given date and time, are referred to collectively as that department's calendar.

Calendared The specific date, time and department for which a case has been set, whether for hearing or trial, is said to have been calendared.

CHP California Highway Patrol

Clocked This term is generally used to describe when an officer gets or determines or observes your speed using whatever method it may be (i.e.: radar, laser, visual, air plane).

Citation Another name for a traffic ticket.

Contest This is a term used to refer to "fighting a ticket".

Correctable Violation This means you can obtain proof of correction and pay a small fee to get rid of the ticket. No traffic school is necessary for a correctable violation.

Courtesy Notice This is the notice sent to you by the court, generally several weeks after you receive the ticket from the officer. The courtesy notice will tell you your options for fighting the ticket, tell you how much the ticket will cost you, and tells you the date by when you must handle the ticket. If you don't receive a courtesy notice you must still contact or appear in court no later than the date listed on your ticket, a courtesy notice is just that, a "courtesy", it's not a mandatory notice that the court MUST send to you.

Dismissal Order or judgment finally disposing of an action, motion, etc.

Entering a Plea When you make a plea to the court you are essentially telling the court whether you did it (guilty), didn't do it (not guilty), or I do not want to say whether or not I did it (no contest).

Failure to Appear This means you didn't take care of your ticket by the deadline. The court can add an additional fee to your original ticket fine or bail and continued failure to comply can result in your case being referred to a collections company, suspension of your driver's license, or a warrant for your arrest.

Infraction This is a term used to describe a minor offense such as a speeding ticket. You can generally only be fined for committing an infraction as compared to being punished by a fine and or jail time for a more serious offense like a misdemeanor.

Laser / Lidar Another type of electronic speed measurement device which is used to pinpoint and pick up the speed of a specific vehicle to which the officer has a clear line of sight. Laser and lidar are used interchangeably, however all California Highway Patrol tickets uses the term lidar whereas a ticket issued by a local city police officer will almost always use the term laser.

Misdemeanor This is a term used to describe a more serious offense such as driving without a license.

MVR Motor Vehicle Record. You can obtain an unofficial copy of your driving record on the CA DMV website for a small fee. http://www.dmv.ca.gov/online/onlinesvcs.htm

Notice to Appear This is the official term used to describe a ticket or citation.

Pace A method used by law enforcement whereby the officer follows another car to estimate the speed.

PD Police Department

Points Points are "demerits" that show up on your California driving record and can cause your license to be revoked or suspended depending on the number of points you have in a given period of time. If you are found guilty of your traffic ticket, traffic infraction or traffic violation, after you pay your fine, additional points may show up on your DMV record unless you can go to traffic school. If the court lets you go to traffic school and you turn in your proof of completion of traffic school to the court before the deadline, the points should not show up on your record. If you get points on your record, for any reason, your insurance company may ask you to pay more for insurance, or they may cancel your policy and tell you to find insurance elsewhere. Points can stay on your record for 3 to 7 years.

Radar A type of electronic speed measurement device which is used to pick up on the speed of the fastest moving target in range. Radar can be used in the stationary or moving mode.

Traffic school If you are found guilty of your traffic ticket, after you pay your fine, points may show up on your DMV record unless you go to traffic school. If the court lets you go to traffic school and you turn in your proof of completion of traffic school to the court before the deadline, the points should not show up on your record. The court can tell you what you need to do to be able to go to traffic school. If this is your first ticket and the court lets you go to traffic school, you should not get any points on your record. In addition to the court fees, the traffic school will also charge you for the class. It will take a whole day to complete. Some courts let you go to traffic school on the web. As long as you have not been to traffic school in the last 18 months and the court honors traffic school for the type of violation you committed, you will get traffic school upon requesting it from the judge. According to Vehicle Code section 42005 and pertaining to *People vs. Wozniak*, you can still have the option to attend traffic school even after you have been found guilty of the alleged violation.

Trial This is when you exercise your right to request an in person court trial with the officer present so you can present your case in front of a judge.

Trial by Declaration (Form TR-205) A way you can fight or contest your ticket in writing without going into court.

Trial De Novo (Form TR-220) If you fight your ticket using a Trial by Declaration and are found guilty then you have the right to request a new trial within 20 days. Trial De Novo means a New Trial and if a Trial De Novo is granted to you it is treated as if no prior trial had been held.

Violation Code This is the number written on the ticket and which usually appears on the courtesy notice as well, and this number represents the offense committed. Generally the letters V and C will appear before the number and these letters don't represent Violation Code, rather they are used to indicate "Vehicle Code" *Example:* VC 22349 (a). This means you were cited for sub section 'a' of section 22349 of the vehicle code and if you were to look up that section you would see that it appears under Speeding over the maximum of 65 mph.

Visual A method used by an officer whereby the officer who is trained to make visual estimations, essentially "eye balls" your speed.